JUST TRUST ME, LOVE GOD

Rodger & Janet Sauls

"Trust in the LORD with all your heart and lean not on your own understanding; in all your ways submit to him, and he will make your paths straight." (Proverbs 3:5-6).

L'Edge Press
PO Box 1652
Boone, NC 28607
ledgepressnc@gmail.com

ISBN: 978-1-935256-91-5

Contact:
Rodger and Janet Sauls

CONTENTS

ACKNOWLEDGEMENTS

We give thanks, praise, glory, and honor to our Lord Jesus Christ for calling Rodger to our marriage ministry and allowing us the opportunity to share with you in this book our experiences of trusting in Him. The entirety of this book is not about marriage or our marriage ministry (2 Become1 Ministries), but rather how our described experiences have affected our marriage in oneness and how they are intertwined within our ministry.

We are deeply grateful to Janet's parents Reverend B. D. and Mildred Stone who are both with our Lord in Heaven. We so much thank them for their love and encouragement of us and our ministry and most of all their fervent prayers over us and our ministry. We appreciate the legacy of Godley parents and being the role models showing us that prayer is the key to everything. We love and miss you both!

We have so much heartfelt appreciation for Rodger's parents Rodger Mack, Sr. and Katrina Sauls who are also both in Heaven with the Lord and were extremely supportive of our ministry. They always felt happy to know we were helping people in their lives and marriages and loved us with all their hearts. We love and miss you both!

How do we even begin to say thanks to our oldest daughter, Heather Beard, and her husband, Reverend Andy Beard, and our youngest daughter, Adrienne Sauls? We offer to each of you our deepest thanks for encouraging us in our ministry and praying for us as we lead retreats and for your encouragement to write this book. Thanks for encouraging us even when we felt we would never get the book to completion and to the publisher. We also appreciate, more than you will ever know, the many hours you gave to help clarify content, share constructive criticism where needed, share ideas for the front book cover and research so much information to help us reach our God-given desire to publishing this book. We love you very much!!!

We extend our sincere and heartfelt gratitude to the New Beginnings Sunday School Class at Shiloh Baptist Church, Garner, North Carolina for their many prayers, support, and encouragement to write our book and their very generous monetary gift to support us with publishing expenses. You are special friends, and we love each of you!!

We owe special thanks to our Editor, Susan Smith, English Professor at Southeastern Baptist Theological Seminary, for her hard work and many hours ensuring our book was edited correctly while trying to meet our aggressive goal to publish before the end of 2020. We have been amazed at her work and so grateful for her expertise.

We express our deepest thanks to our Publisher, Mr. Jeff Hendley and his graphic designer, Abbie Frease, L'edge Press, who worked diligently to ensure we met our goal of publishing our book as close to the end of 2020 as possible. We could not have asked for anyone better to work with us to get everything accomplished.

We owe our gratitude to Mr. Kirk Pullen, Kirk Pullen Photography, Mount Olive, NC. He willingly and graciously gave of his time and efforts to meticulously design, per special request, the front cover of our book in record time to help us meet our publish goal date!

We give an extra special thank you to Dr. Allan Moseley, Senior Professor of Old Testament and Hebrew, Southeastern Baptist Theological Seminary, and to Dr. Mark Smith, Senior Consultant, Family Evangelism and Discipleship at the Baptist State Convention of North Carolina for their recommendations of various editors and publishers. We appreciate their insightful comments and suggestions regarding publishing our book.

PREFACE

Over the last 44 years of marriage, we have enjoyed great mountaintop experiences as a couple and with family: our own marriage, births of two beautiful and precious daughters, remarriage of our oldest daughter, and the births of two handsome and fun-loving grandsons. However, we have also lived through some of the valleys of life: sickness, deaths and grief, accidents, sadness, selfishness, pouting, divorce within the family, loss of jobs, and being caregivers. By the grace and mercy of God and His forgiveness, we are still very much in love, and we still want to enjoy each other and life together. We are both simple people; it does not take much to make us happy. Just a walk outside to share a cup of coffee and looking at how much the flowers have grown or how good the fresh cut grass looks and smells each week, an occasional dinner out somewhere quiet, sharing our thoughts and plans, and walking through a mall hand in hand sometimes shopping but sometimes just looking are some of the simple things we enjoy together. Simple but warming. We all need to slow down and smell the roses, communicate, get to really know each other and reacquaint ourselves with each other. Marriage takes lots of hard work and dedication. Oh, and Rodger says it was fun when we had a boat and enjoyed family together; maybe we will again someday!

Life is full of heartaches and trials even for Christians. In life's challenges and disappointments, we need to trust God fully, which is not always easy. It is much easier to trust Him when we are on the mountaintop. When we look back on the hard times and the sad times and see God's faithfulness to us, we need to be grateful. We need to trust Him every day and depend on Him 100%! Even though there are days we feel weak, we need to remember, He is strong. "Tis So Sweet to Trust in Jesus", "The Unseen Hand," and "Trust and Obey" are old songs that remind us to trust Him.

We are very aware that there are many of you reading this book who have experienced better or more exciting and higher mountains as well as worse and lower valleys. There are so many things we have not had the pleasure or misfortune of experiencing, but this book contains the experiences God has given us to grow our faith in Him and share with others. After each mountaintop experience, we have given God praise and glory. During the valleys, we have tried to continue giving God praise and glory and trust even more. Sometimes we have felt like failures at trusting God, but He has always been faithful. Those are the faith builder moments when we can look back over the valleys and the mountains in our life and see God's faithfulness and His timing in all things. These moments give us courage and strength to continue placing our trust and faith in Jesus Christ each day!

****

In this book, we have provided scripture for both study and reflection. All scripture shared is taken from The New International Version of The Holy Bible.

CHAPTER 1

The Call to Marriage Ministry

We will never forget the day that our oldest child broke the news to us that marriage trials pushed her and her husband to separate from their vows. That was in March 2004, when winter was almost over, and the bright sunny days of spring were on the horizon. The only problem was that it did not feel so bright or that winter would ever end. Their divorce was finalized in 2005.

We are aware of what the Bible says about divorce. Though the divorce met the Biblical criteria for permissible divorce, we were still crushed and devastated. Our hearts were heavy because we know that Malachi 2:16 shares God's anger for divorce, "I hate divorce, says the Lord God of Israel."

We know that God created marriage to reflect His character and unconditional love. Divorce is the tearing apart of the two who became one after God joined them together. However, we need to **always remember** that **God loves the divorcee** because he or she is heart-broken and needs God's healing love. The separation and divorce were both very painful and devastating, but we totally trusted God and leaned fully on Him and His promises.

****

"And so we know and rely on the love God has for us. God is love. Whoever lives in love lives in God, and God in him." (1 John 4:16).

****

****

"The Lord himself goes before you and will be with you; He will never leave you nor forsake you. Do not be afraid; do not be discouraged." (Deuteronomy 31:8).

****

Rodger's Story

In February 2004, I had a very real experience with God. Nothing like this had ever happened to me before, and it has not happened since. Janet was in the bathroom getting ready for work, and I was still in bed getting ready to get up and shower. I was much awake and aware. I knew in my heart and mind that God was urging me to do something but was unaware of the task. I wrestled within myself while I asked God, "What is it you want me to do?" Still, there was no answer, but I said *no* in my head and heart. As I tried to get out of bed, I could not move. I tried to call out to Janet and could not speak. Even though I did not understand what was happening, I felt peace. God was asking me to do something; what was it? I did not want to do whatever it might be, did I? Well, I certainly did not want to be a paralyzed mute for the remainder of my life, so I said, "God, okay! Whatever you want me to do, I will do it!" Immediately, I could move and speak. Later, I explained to Janet what I had experienced but had no idea of God's plans.

Over the next several months, as I traveled out of town to Asheville, North Carolina, which was my job territory, I typically listened to WMIT, The Light, a Billy

Graham radio station. One day, I heard Jimmy Evans speaking about a book he and his wife had written, *Marriage on the Rock*. They were offering a free book with the purchase of their CDs. That was it! God confirmed in my heart that is what He wanted me to do: a ministry for marriages! I shared with Janet that I needed her help because I believed God wanted a couple sharing with couples what God's Word says about marriage. Janet asked, "What?! *Me?!*"

Janet's Story

I looked Rodger in the face and told him there was no way I could help anyone without first helping myself. Up to that point in our marriage, I had dealt with issues of self-esteem. My issues began when I was a child and began affecting me more after marriage. I am sure no one reading this book has ever dealt with or has ever known anyone with self-esteem issues, right? *Wrong!* We are aware it is a common issue. Previously, I never wanted to discuss my issues with a counselor or anyone even at the urging of my sweet husband because it might make me seem, well, imperfect. Oh, by the way, we are all imperfect and will not be perfected until we are home with Jesus. Our daughter went to see a wonderful and professional counselor after her separation, so I decided to have a few chats with her myself. After a few conversations, I realized I had all the confidence I needed because I am a child of the King! *His royal blood flows through my veins, and that makes me a princess!* Because I was a pastor's kid, I already knew this, but God had to bring me to the point to openly admit my esteem problem before he could help me. We all need to be willing to admit to ourselves that we need help before we can begin to let God help and heal us. I had to take a good look in the mirror and ask myself why I pouted with Rodger when his comments hurt my feelings. Why did I wear my feelings on my sleeve with him? As Rodger will tell you, he is a straight shooter, as there is no grey within his viewpoint. He tells it like it is, so to speak. With my feelings on my sleeve, he occasionally said things that seemed harsh to me, but he did not mean it to be ugly or hurtful; he just spoke plain language. I learned over the last 16 years to take my feelings off my sleeve and ask him to translate his comments so that I do not take those the wrong way. We discuss his comments and come to an understanding of the content. Over the years, I have not felt the need to waste time any longer pouting to let him know he hurt my feelings. We now communicate. That works much better and saves so much pain, agony, and time. We have found that forgiveness is always an appropriate action for us which works both ways, asking and receiving.

Rodger's Story

Janet and I both believe that through our daughter's separation and divorce and typical issues we were having in our own marriage, God used these events to call me to help others regarding marriage. God can use the bad for good *if* we are willing. Initially, as Janet explained, she felt very unequipped to help anyone and that she needed help herself, but God is like that, as He can use those who feel inadequate. I felt the same way. *How was I going to do this?* We began to pray and read God's Word for His plan for Godly marriages.

Janet's Story

Over the next two years, we prayed, studied the Bible, and read many Biblical based books about marriage. Through many prayers over us and our ministry, God gave me more strength than I ever imagined possible to fight the old inner self telling me I could not do this task! I was ready to face other couples because God called Rodger, and I am his helpmate. God had brought us to this appointed time in our lives, and I was READY! We trusted and still trust God!

****

After two years of preparation, in 2006, we started facilitating 11-week marriage classes and leading marriage retreats at our church and at other churches in North Carolina as well as out-of-state. Also, at that time, we began lay ministry pre-marriage counseling and marriage counseling. Because we are not trained as licensed professional counselors, we have always understood our boundaries especially when dealing with certain issues such as PTSD or other psychological issues. However, we are always happy to share God's Word with couples about His plan for marriage. Also, in 2010, the Baptist State Convention of North Carolina began sending us to churches who requested marriage retreats. Through that painful divorce in 2005 and issues we faced in our own marriage, God birthed "2 Become 1 Ministries" which is still alive and well.

Today, we truly are trusting God for the next steps and for the path He would have us take for our marriage ministry. We ask our readers to please say a prayer for us that we will do exactly as God intends for us related to our ministry.

****

"But I trust in you, O Lord; I say",
"You, are my God." (Psalm 31:14).

****

Study and Reflection

- Whenever you are struggling in your marriage, as we all do from to time, do you trust God enough to let him take control? Do you seek His guidance and His will for your relationship through God's Word, Christian pastors, Christian counselors, or other Godly mentors or, do you seek advice from the world? Do you fully trust God's will for your own life?

- Does your marriage sometimes feel chaotic or full of confusion?

- 1 Cor. 14:33 reminds us that God does not create anything chaotic and without order, for He is not a God of confusion. Prayerfully ask Him to show you what is missing or what needs to change in your marriage.

- Do you struggle with issues of low self-esteem? In Galatians 3:26, the Bible tell us that if we are saved by Jesus Christ through our faith, we are children of God. So, ladies, if you are a child of the King, that makes you a princess! Guys, that makes you royalty as well. The Bible also tells women in Proverbs 31:25 that if we are a wife of noble character, we are clothed in strength and dignity.

- Do you struggle with a self-esteem that is too high that might cause you to be arrogant or have a feeling of superiority? 2 Timothy 3:1-5 warns us about being conceited or boastful.

- If you struggle with either of these esteem issues, have you prayerfully trusted God to help you?

CHAPTER 2

70-Times-7= Forgiveness

Sometimes, certainly not always, we can be depressed because of unforgiveness in our hearts. Our hearts can become consumed with bitterness, resentment, or sin. Unforgiveness can paralyze us! Also, anger turned inward can sometimes cause depression. In Matthew 18:21-35, God's Word tell us that we need to be forgiving servants. Peter asked Jesus how many times he should forgive those who sin against him. Jesus told Peter that he should forgive them seventy times seven. We should apply that verse to our own lives so that we share unlimited forgiveness to others. God forgives us as often as we ask; therefore, we should trust God to forgive us of our sins and any negative attributes, like bitterness and resentment.

A man who impressed Matthew 18 upon our hearts was Janet's dad, B. D. Stone, who was born in 1930, married in 1950, and surrendered his life to Christ in 1953. He was a devoted Christian, prayer warrior, and was called to preach in 1955. He was an evangelist for many years throughout North Carolina, and he also served as pastor at a small church in Kenly, North Carolina and led a church plant in Spring Hope, North Carolina.

****

"If we confess our sins, He is faithful and just and will forgive us our sins and purify us from all unrighteousness." (1 John 1:9).

****

****

"For if you forgive men when they sin against you, your heavenly Father will also forgive you. But if you do not forgive men their sins, your Father will not forgive your sins." (Matthew 6:14-15).

****

In 1993, Dad felt a special urging of God's Spirit to create something about forgiveness (70-TIMES-7) which is clearly described in the Bible as stated at the beginning of this chapter. He purchased sheets of aluminum and had a business owner create a similar replica of his personal license plate that depicted 70-TIMES-7 and looked like the typical North Carolina license plate. Dad proudly and humbly displayed it on the front of his truck and loved for folks to ask him its meaning. That little license plate replica became a conversation piece to anyone who asked, and Dad explained that Jesus died on the cross to save us from our sins. He further shared that God wants us to ask Him for forgiveness to be saved from sin and to ask God's forgiveness every day afterwards. Also, God wants us to ask all those in our lives to forgive us when needed. That includes our spouse, children, coworkers, neighbors, family members, church members, and the hard-to-deal with people at the shopping mall, golf course or hunting tree stand…even before they ask. Dad said just try to think of a single relationship that we do not need forgiveness. Then, we need to be willing to forgive others when they ask (and even when they do not ask). Last, but not least, we must be willing to forgive ourselves. Dad said so many people go through life forgiven by God and others but never forgive themselves. As a result, they live very unhappy, depressed lives.

Dad told folks that is what the license plate means and represents, so we need to get it up, get it out, put it behind ourselves, get over it, and forget it! Dad told people that it would work for them day and night; while they worked, ate, and even while they slept. He believed it was an ideal addition to assist ministers, teachers, marriage counselors, or anyone. Dad encouraged everyone to put a 70-times-7 reminder somewhere they would see it every day: on the front of their vehicle, in their office, on their trailer or boat, in their repair shop, waiting room, on their den mantle, or on a mirror they can see when they look at themselves. He felt this forgiveness message might help all of us have our prayers answered and gain Heaven. Because **HE LIVES**, we can live in freedom through forgiveness! Little did we know that this license plate would later be an integral part of our marriage ministry!

My dad sold the license plates over the years to many people, and we have sold them at our marriage classes and retreats over the last 14 years. Also, there are times we have given the license plates as gifts. One evening, I spoke at a ladies' event and planned to give one of the plates as a door prize. I prayed that whichever lady needed the gift most would be the one to receive it that evening. After the event, one of the ladies came up to me crying stating that she hated her dad, and she goes to bed every night starring at the ceiling with feelings of hate. She said she would place the license plate on the ceiling as a reminder to forgive. Another gentleman we gave the gift to stated he would place it on his mantle where he passed each day as a reminder to not have negative and unforgiving feelings about his ex-wife. Rodger and I spoke to a man who had serious depression problems. He told us he had a bad relationship with his dad and had a tremendous amount of resentment for things that had happened as he was growing up and even as an adult. We gave him a license plate and explained the 70-TIMES-7 concept and how it has healing effects on our heart and life. Over the years, we have shared the gift with many people who were hurting and needed forgiveness in their lives and pray it made a positive impact.

God loves us and has a plan for our lives. John 3:16 shares a message of genuine love, "For God so loved the world that he gave His one and only Son, that whoever believes in Him shall not perish but have eternal life." God's invitation to us is found in Revelation 3:20, "Here I am! I stand at the door and knock. If anyone hears my voice and opens the door, I will come in and eat with him, and he with me." We need to let that sink into our hearts and know the door to God's invitation is always with an open door.

****

If the following prayer expresses the desire of your heart, you can pray this prayer and Jesus Christ will come into your life as He has promised, and you will obtain the gift of salvation.

Dear Jesus,
I know that I am a sinner and in need of forgiveness.
I believe that you died for my sins and rose again.
I want to turn from my sins and invite you into my heart and life as my Lord
and Savior. In Jesus' Name, Amen.

****

"For it is by grace you have been saved, through faith-and this not from yourselves, it is the gift of God." (Ephesians 2:8).

****

Study and Reflection

-   Forgiveness is not easy. Is there someone you need to forgive, and that may include yourself for regrettable decisions from your past? If so, take these four steps to freedom from the burden you are carrying:

    a. Pray that God will give you the strength and courage to forgive

    b. Let the person know they are forgiven.

    c. Reinforce your forgiveness with your behavior

    d. Trust God to allow you to forget and renew your mind with new attitudes

-   Those who do not choose to forgive can experience bitterness and become crippled emotionally by their feelings, which ultimately prevents them from walking in personal fellowship with God. If you are feeling separated from God due to unforgiveness, you can change all of that today. Begin by asking God to forgive you for your sins and then follow the steps above to begin the restoration process with one or more people in your life. By making this decision your life will be changed forever. Make note of today's date and the person(s) you have chosen to forgive. Even if the person does not accept the forgiveness, at least you will restore your relationship with God.

CHAPTER 3

Somebody Listen to Me!

A "Moment" from Rodger

One day, many years ago, when our girls were small, they had a "moment" of not being good listeners. They had pushed all of Janet's internal elevator's buttons and reached her highest floor of patience. Janet is a relatively patient and sweet person; however, that "moment" of our girls' elevator ride to the top floor was enough! I think Janet was also trying to be funny, as she does sometimes even now, but at that "moment," it was hard to determine. Janet jumped up on the kitchen counter and looked down at the three of us. She knew how to gain our undivided attention. She became the queen of our kitchen and chitter-chatter stopped when we noticed her seriousness. Janet exclaimed, "SOMEBODY LISTEN TO ME!" At that moment, we could have heard a pin drop. Her face did not crack a smile, and as far as we knew, this was not a playful moment. Our ears were open, and seriousness abounded. Janet wanted our attention, and she got it!

Just as Janet wanted our attention and poised herself to get it, there were many days that I wanted somebody -- *anybody* -- to listen to me. I wanted to tell one million plus people at the same time about what we have learned over the last 16 years that God's Word says to us about marriage. God, though, had a different plan. He revealed that the plan is for us to share with a few couples at a time, at least right now, so we trust Him with this calling that is not our own. It is His.

In the early part of 2014, God laid it on Janet's heart that we needed to write a book, and on March 2, 2014, God gave her part of the title, *Just Trust Me*, and as soon as she told me, I said, "Love God." So, here we are, and this is the title! Though the progression of fulfilling this calling to complete the book has taken some time, mostly due to life's events, we have finally made this happen. We have devoted a special chapter to speak more about doing what God asks us to do and not make excuses.

Hopefully, this book will enable us to reach even more people about God, His faithfulness, His plan for marriage, and trusting in Him! We will not try to reprint the awesome information explaining marriage already written in countless books written by each of the well-known Christian authors, but we know our unique stories may be a blessing for the ones who hold this book. There are some questions we can reflect upon to make us aware of how we live our daily lives together.

As you read our stories, we ask that you reflect on your own marriage.

Ask yourself: Do you...

- *communicate regularly with your spouse?*
- *wake up each morning thinking what you can do to make your spouse's day better?*
- *view your marriage relationship as permanent?*
- *understand and meet each other's sexual needs?*
- *love and/or respect your spouse?*
- *behave selfishly or selflessly?*
- *spend more time on social media or playing games than with your family?*
- *spend quality time with your spouse and/or family?*

- *do your best for each other?*

- *have and adhere to a budget?*

- *make significant financial decisions together?*

- *understand your spouse's basic needs and differences?*

- *still have date nights and/or days?*

- *live a life of purity?*

- *trust God when there seems to be no way?*

- *trust that He will supply all your needs (not necessarily wants)?*

- *pray together?*

- *have a personal relationship with Jesus?*

The last reflection question is the most important aspect of a person's life or marriage relationship. It is much easier to walk in oneness with your spouse when each of you know and love Jesus Christ and are both dedicated to serving Him wholly. After all, He is the Creator of marriage and wants to be part of yours. Life and marriage go better with Him at the center. Let go of the grip of whatever it is that has control over you and trust Him with every situation of your life and your marriage, not just in this "moment" but forever. The more you each seek God, the closer you become to Him and the closer you grow together obtaining the oneness of His perfect design.

Study and Reflection

- Do you remember a time when you responded to the urge to accept Jesus as your personal Savior? Is your relationship with Jesus Christ your priority in life? If not, what changes do you need to make? If so, how do you show that He is your priority to your family?

- Remember that others are watching how you live your life. Do you want your children or those who are engaged to have a marriage just like yours? If the answer is yes, wonderful. If the answer is no, ask yourself why not and what you need to do differently?

- Have you achieved the level of oneness in your marriage desired by God? His design is perfect, but as humans, we are not perfect. Marriage, while striving for oneness, is something we need to work at every day. Ask yourself what do I need to do to be more Christlike in my marriage?

CHAPTER 4

Trust God in the Mountaintop Experiences and in the Valleys of Life

Let me (Janet) take you for a "ride" through some of our mountaintop and valley journeys we have traveled over our years of marriage. All couples and individuals deal with happy days and sad days, but we must remember our joy comes from Jesus and not from our routine surroundings or people as those events cause happiness or sadness. Someone once said that JOY is **J**esus first, **O**thers next and **Y**ou last. That is so true! We must remember to trust God in the valleys as well as on the mountaintops!

Rodger and I met in college in February 1976, engaged in April 1976, and married on October 16, 1976. We certainly did not waste time, did we? That year of forming a relationship to joining in marriage was a definite mountaintop experience! We were so in love! We knew we were right for each other from the start! Rodger worked at a local restaurant in high school and college, and he had seen me there with my family on several occasions. He had also seen me on campus and had asked some of my friends everything about me and my family, so he was familiar with me before we met. He was a freshman, and I was a sophomore. (Yes, I am eight months older than him.) Rodger was a full-time student and worked full-time at the restaurant, sometimes over 60 hours a week. He managed to make time for me every single evening, other than one when he was out of town catering a party. Did we know anything about marriage? No! When we married in October 1976, Rodger had three years of college ahead of him, and I was ready for a family right away! We had a three-day honeymoon while Rodger was on fall break.

Obviously, I was a born nurturer because at the age of nine or ten, I wanted my very own baby! At that age, I was naïve and did not know how babies were conceived or how they were born, but I wanted one. On July 23, 1978, our first child was born, and what a beautiful little girl with red, fuzzy hair! We were so happy and could hardly contain our mountaintop excitement! After many sleepless nights, busy work schedules, and a busy school schedule for Rodger, reality became clear: we had a baby, and we were parents!

What would happen next on our journey through life together? We were probably like most young parents; we learned over time. Each day, we grew into parenthood and learned there are no perfect parents. It is funny how over time, people forget the childbirth pain, the sleepless nights, the poopy diapers, the spit up, the crying, and the worrying during their sicknesses.

God blessed us again on August 10, 1982 with the birth of our second child, another beautiful girl with blond, fuzzy hair. (There seems to be a theme of the fuzz, doesn't it? Maybe it is a symbol of how fuzzy time can seem when we look through the rear-view mirror to see how swiftly those years passed!) As with the birth of our first born, we were so excited with our new family addition, and it was easy to be back on the mountaintop. Our oldest was four years old when our second baby was born, and she was such a great helper; however, two was much more time consuming than we expected. They were such good girls and so sweet. They were not perfect kids, but we all know there is no such thing as perfection on this side of heaven.

My nurturing instincts kicked in big time, and I found it hard to leave for work each day. I wanted to spend every minute with the girls when I was home from my job. Sometimes, I felt guilty for not staying home with them, but with Rodger in school full-time and working full-time, I did not feel it was prudent to give up my job to stay home. We needed that little extra income my paycheck provided, or so we thought.

Rodger and I always had time together, enjoyed each other, and loved each other, but the girls went with us everywhere. We never had date night. What was that? I felt so badly about leaving them during the day, I did not want to leave them at nights and weekends, so we did not do much without them being with us. One day when the girls were maybe four and eight years old, Rodger explained to me that he felt second fiddle to the girls. "What?!" I exclaimed! How could that be? I always spent time with him. He explained that he did not want to sound selfish, but he felt the girls were my priority over him. Was that possible? Was I placing more importance on our girls than my husband? The Bible is clear in Genesis that in the beginning was God, then marriage was created between Adam and Eve, and then children were born to them. Obviously, my priorities were out of order. While there were times in our lives when our young children needed to take precedence, especially when they were sick, hungry, or needed a clean diaper, I may have gone overboard and left my husband out of the picture without realizing the proper order of my God-given priorities.

Over time, I made changes, and we began having date nights. Let me be clear. It was not an easy transition for me, the nurturer. The first time we left home to go away for one night without our girls, we stopped to get gas, and I was crying so hard that Rodger took me back home. That is just over the top pitiful on my part, but it is a true story of our parenting adventure, and one I am not proud to share. However, if this part of our experience is helpful to one Mom who needs to leave her child for a date night, then okay. We were young and did not make all the right decisions. We can now say that we "should have done this and should have done that," but unfortunately, we did not then. After some time, the girls became involved in youth group and other activities, and it became much easier to leave them. It was about time, right?! Then came college and moving away from home for the girls. The first year of leaving each daughter at college was tough; Mom cried, and Dad's heart was heavy. Now, as they are grown, we love for our girls to come home, we love our time together with them, and Rodger and I also love our empty nest!

Mountaintop experiences in our journey through life are awesome, but life also consists of valley experiences along the way. On October 31,1987, Rodger spent the morning with his dad using his truck to get pine straw. After completing the task together, Rodger headed to the driving range for golf practice and realized he had left a pair of glasses on the front seat of his dad's truck. Rodger called his dad to let him know he was coming back to pick up his glasses later that afternoon, and his dad said he would be home. Afterwards, Rodger headed back to his dad's, and while in route, he noticed billowing smoke in the distance. He continued to his dad's but found he was not home. Little did Rodger know the rising smoke he witnessed moments earlier was his dad's truck in a horrific accident. I was home and on the telephone with my mom when our conversation was cut short by the operator telling me that due to an emergency, we needed to end our conversation. Law enforcement alerted me on the telephone there had been an accident involving Rodger's dad and he needed to go to the hospital. Soon after the telephone conversation ended, Rodger returned home, and I gave him the news. We found out his dad had left his home after working with Rodger to have a propane tank filled for a recently purchased gas grill. It was an unusually warm Halloween day with temperatures exceeding 80 degrees. Because Mr. Sauls had no safe way to secure the tank in the back of his pickup truck, he placed the tank inside the cab on the passenger's seat. While traveling home, the tank unexpectedly began to expel gas, likely because it was overfilled. Accident reconstruction experts speculated that an electrical arc from an undetermined origin, possibly the air conditioner, caused the gas to ignite engulfing the cab with flames. Even as the truck cab was full of flames, instincts took over as Mr. Sauls stopped the vehicle, placed it in park, and attempted to reach over and open the passenger door to remove the tank from the truck. Due to having on his seatbelt, he was unable to reach the passenger door handle. He then cut off the engine and removed the keys. We were able to reconstruct some of this information due to his keys being found melted into the pavement of the road. He got out of the truck and did the "stop, drop, and roll" technique we have always been taught. His truck was completely burned, and he received third degree burns over 60% of his body. Rodger went to meet his mom initially at WakeMed Hospital Raleigh and was also allowed to see his dad briefly. Walking into the trauma bay, even with 60% of his body burned, Rodger's dad looked at him and said, "I guess your glasses are gone." Shortly thereafter, his dad was transported, via ambulance, to the North Carolina Jaycee Burn Center in Chapel Hill.

During this horrific time, we received news that was hard to hear. When Rodger arrived at the hospital, the head of the Burn Center told him he needed to prepare for his dad's death because the chances of his survival through the night were slim due to his age and percentage of burns. This was one of life's valleys for sure, but God…He had other plans.

****

"My help comes from the Lord, the Maker of Heaven and earth." (Psalm 121:2).

****

Along our journey, we learned patience during a long hospitalization for Rodger's dad. He stayed at the Burn Center for two and a half months and came home mid-January despite inclement weather due to snow and ice. Rodger was determined to get his dad home no matter the weather. Rodger and his dad were discharged and quickly escaped down a rear stairwell with his dad wrapped in a blanket to get ahead of the worsening driving conditions. His dad had endured painful treatment, multiple surgeries, and was badly scarred, but he was alive. It is impossible to give all the details of his experience, but we know that it was not fun for him, and he did not talk much about the day of his event. He continued to have a great attitude considering all he had experienced, which taught us a lesson itself on this adventure we are traveling together through life.

Trusting in God is easy on the good days, but during challenges, especially those involving our children, our faith can be tested. We were extremely blessed that neither of our children experienced major childhood disease, accidents, or issues. All parents are faced at some point with difficult situations that, if we are not careful, can be a distraction from our walk with the Lord.

One difficulty we faced was when our youngest daughter, Adrienne, had a history of ear infections beginning in infancy and required multiple sets of tubes. In the fall of 1989, after a fun summer of swimming, Adrienne developed a serious issue with swimmer's ear. During a visit to her ENT physician, he discovered a hole on her eardrum, and after taking a closer look, she was diagnosed with a Cholesteatoma in her right ear. Praise God for a thorough physician who was diligent to find an answer to her problem. A cholesteatoma is a growth of skin, a cyst that occurs in an unusual location, the middle ear behind the eardrum. Over time, the Cholesteatoma increases in size and can destroy the nearby bones of the middle ear. If left untreated, this bone erosion can cause the infection to spread to the surrounding areas including the skull, and eventually the brain, potentially resulting in deafness, brain abscess, meningitis, and, in rare cases, death can occur. The ENT indicated that the Cholesteatoma would need to be removed surgically which is not something any parent wants to hear.

Even with young school age children, finding a time for surgery and recovery can be challenging. Because of the timing of Adrienne's diagnosis, the best available time for her *first* surgery was the week after Christmas and prior to classes reconvening in January. To limit the invasiveness of the surgery, the surgeon planned to remove the Cholesteatoma through the ear canal while also attaching a skin graft to her injured eardrum. Adrienne had a relatively quick recovery and got along well following the procedure. What a blessing it was, especially for a young child and her worried parents! However, that was not the ending for this difficult adventure. The cholesteatoma was in a difficult location, and after several months of rechecks, her surgically repaired eardrum once again developed a hole because the cyst had returned and ruined the initial skin graft. It became evident that a *second* surgery would be required. Once again, Adrienne was scheduled for surgery during the Christmas holiday break. Unfortunately, this time the procedure was more invasive and required an incision from top to bottom on the backside of the ear.

This enabled the surgeon to lay the ear forward while gaining much greater access to the affected area inside. The recuperation was more extended and required several months for the swelling to completely subside. Our hearts ached for Adrienne, when at eight years old, she looked in the mirror and said with tears, "I look like dumbo!" God was again faithful and provided Adrienne with full recovery from her ordeal.

That was not the end of this journey, though. To be sure the Cholesteatoma was not returning, a much less invasive exploratory surgery was required in September of the following year. Thankfully, we were able to avoid the Christmas holidays for this third surgery. Despite the surgeon's best efforts and due to the graft becoming more rigid than a normal eardrum, Adrienne did sustain significant hearing loss in that ear. The blessing through all of this is that God allowed a talented doctor to diagnose and treat an issue that had the potential to do even greater damage. Praise Jesus!

Over the years, most of our family trips were limited to destinations that involved car travel, but occasionally we took longer trips involving air travel. During the winter of 1993, we spent time planning our first snow ski trip to Colorado. Rodger learned to ski later in life and wanted to experience fresh powder as opposed to the icier conditions found in much of the eastern United States. It seemed to make the falls and spills much less painful. Hoping for smaller crowds and lower lift ticket prices, we targeted the first week in April during spring break for our first great adventure on the slopes of the Rocky Mountains.

God speaks to us in different ways, and He sent us somewhat of a warning regarding our trip, although we did not recognize it as such at the time. Two weeks prior to our trip to Winter Park, Colorado, Heather developed the flu. As with many flu patients, she spent several days out of school recuperating and keeping up with her studies as best as possible. She went back to school on Monday and felt well the entire week ahead of our ski trip. We departed the next Sunday morning and had a great trip to Denver and enjoyed the beautiful drive to the Winter Park Resort.

The next morning, with skis and boots in hand, Rodger and the girls set out for the slopes. I am not a skier, so I decided to spend time at the lodge enjoying the fireplace, the view, and reading a good book. I also spent time praying for the three who were skiing. Eventually, my family of snow skiers came back to the lodge for lunch. What a great time we had. Heather and Rodger decided to go back for more time on the slopes, while Adrienne stayed with me to rest and watch television. Heather asked if she and Rodger could try out a different slope. The drop off point for that lift was above 11,000 feet and higher than any trail they skied earlier in the day. Talk about an adventure! The next hour proved to be interesting and unexpected.

As they began to ski down, Heather, a much better skier than Rodger, began to get winded and complained she was out of breath. Rodger's initial reaction was that she was probably feeling extra excitement of the higher altitude, or maybe simply adjusting to the thinner air, so they took it slow, stopping to rest periodically, and eventually made it to the base of the mountain. They agreed to call it a day and made their way back to the condo. Following some rest time, we headed out for an early dinner with plans to come back and watch the Finals of the NCAA Men's Basketball Tournament later that evening. While at dinner, Heather began to get emotional and indicated that her chest felt like she was getting the flu again. We were concerned and went back to our condo to allow her to rest. As the evening progressed, we discovered Heather had a rising temperature. We contacted a local clinic, and they recommended we give her Tylenol and watch her fever overnight, and unless the fever got above 103 degrees, they would see her the next morning when the clinic reopened. The Tylenol seemed to work over night, and the fever remained under 103 degrees.

Early the next morning, Heather's condition began to go downhill – no pun intended. Around 8:00 AM, her fever spiked to 104.5 and we headed to the clinic. As soon as they opened, they saw Heather immediately because of her deteriorating condition. The staff indicated they were concerned that she may be dealing with altitude sickness. As they began to check her vital signs, they attempted to get a blood pressure while she laid on the examination table. They were unable to get a blood pressure reading, so they had her sit up and tried again. Heather's blood pressure was only 60/30 – *not good*! The next step was a chest x-ray which showed one of her lungs was quickly filling with fluid. The final diagnosis was bacterial pneumonia which was most likely a secondary infection from her earlier sickness with the flu. The situation was extremely serious, and they told us she needed to be admitted to a hospital as soon as possible. They started a powerful intravenous antibiotic and called for a rescue vehicle. Soon after, Heather and I were on our way down the mountain to the hospital in Denver. Adrienne and Rodger returned to the condo, packed everyone's belongings for the three-day ski trip, and made the drive to Denver, not fully knowing what to expect when they arrived. Our entire family prayed continually during that trip for a positive outcome.

When Adrienne and Rodger arrived at the hospital in Denver around midday on Tuesday, they were reassured by hospital staff that Heather was going to be okay! Thank you, Lord! Heather remained in the hospital for three days, and we were able to return home on Friday! What a journey through an uncertain time! **Just trust me, love God!**

Several years after the birth of our first daughter, I began having hives and the doctor thought I might be allergic to a food or laundry detergent; however, after making changes, the hives were still present over the years. I continued having various outbreaks of hives to the point of experiencing them in my ears, nose, and throat. Twice,

I ended up at the emergency room to have shots. Due to my white blood count being so low, I was sent to Rex Cancer Center in Raleigh to see a cancer specialist to determine if I had Leukemia. After six months of testing and waiting, I was told that if my blood count became lower, I would need to be hospitalized to determine the cause, but praise the Lord, I did not have Leukemia! These weird uncomfortable health issues continued for years.

After a second episode of pericarditis, which is inflammation around the heart, my cardiologist had a suspicion and sent me to a rheumatologist to be tested. In June 1996, just before my 40th Birthday, I, was diagnosed with Systemic Lupus, which is a chronic inflammatory and sometimes disabling auto-immune disease which can affect almost any organ or system in one's body. My rheumatologist determined that I probably had Lupus for 10-12 years prior to that visit. After my doctor's visit, I walked to my car feeling sort of numb and really did not have a clue about Lupus. The doctor had given me information to share with my family. During my sick days, I still felt positive and trusted in the Lord. It is very humbling to be so sick.

Initially, I only shared my news with Rodger, and not even our girls, our parents, or our church family knew of my illness. However, after a year of sickness, I felt it was time to share with everyone. I told our girls and our parents, and my name was placed on the church prayer list. I felt a bit guilty since there were so many other people with worse health issues, and I did not really have the physical appearance of being sick. No one could tell I felt bad. Unless I told someone, they had no idea I was experiencing this disease. I continued to work even though there were days I was extremely tired and took a few naps in my car during lunch hour. I even remember taking a short siesta on a table in an empty conference room. It was hard to hold my head up some days after work to take care of our two children, but God provided. Through all of this, I was determined to be the happiest Lupus patient ever.

Even though I had been taking medication prescribed by my rheumatologist, by October of 1998, I was still sick. I had now developed Chronic Obstructive Pulmonary Disease (COPD) and found it difficult to breathe, talk, exercise, climb stairs, and even sing in the church choir. My skin, blood, heart, and lungs had been affected along with symptoms of fatigue and joint pain. After the Christmas cantata in December of 1998, I determined I needed to be out of the choir for an indefinite time. I told our worship leader that even though I could not sing, I could still pray, and I would be praying for him, his wife, and the entire choir. Each Sunday as I sat in the pew, tears rolled down my cheeks as I had been singing since the age of three and singing at that church for 16 years. Singing is in my blood and my heart. During the time out of choir, I prayed very intensely for the choir director, his wife, and the choir and continued trusting in the Lord. My faith was still strong though my body was weak. Also, I began reading a list of scriptures my dad had given me. The scriptures were "faith builders" and God's promises.

These are a few of those scriptures:

****

"Praise the LORD, O my soul; all my inmost being, praise his holy name. Praise the LORD, O my soul, and forget not all his benefits-who forgives all your sins and heals all your diseases, who redeems your life from the pit and crowns you with love and compassion, who satisfies your desires with good things so that your youth is renewed like the eagle's." (Psalm 103:1-5).

****

****

"Therefore I tell you, whatever you ask for in prayer, believe that you have received it, and it will be yours." (Mark 11:24).

****

****

"Consequently, faith comes from hearing the message, and the message is heard through the word of Christ." (Romans 10:17).

****

****

"Is anyone of you in trouble? He should pray. Is anyone happy? Let him sing songs of praise. Is anyone among you sick? He should call the elders of the church to pray over him and anoint him with oil in the name of the Lord. And the prayer offered in faith will make the sick person well; the Lord will raise him up. If he has sinned, he will be forgiven. Therefore, confess your sins to each other and pray for each other so that you may be healed. The prayer of a righteous man is powerful and effective." (James 5:13-16).

****

There were many other scriptures that my dad shared with me to help me find joy in the trials and trust in God by faith. Dad told me to read these scriptures every day and take them in as nourishment like I was taking my vitamins, exercising, eating healthy, and praying. Most definitely, I was praying faithfully and asking God to help me so I could go back to choir and sing and be healthy again. My faith was great, and I continued trusting God.

On Sunday, January 31, 1999, our pastor, Dr. Jeff Beckett preached his acceptance sermon at Salem Baptist Church in Apex, North Carolina. His scripture text was from Joshua Chapter 3. He talked about faith and trusting God. The generation of Joshua had faith, and they were ready to step into the water even though the rivers waters were at flood level. Pastor Beckett said, "You are ready to plunge by faith when every challenge looks possible. You step into the water, and God will do His part." Health was my challenge. Being raised in a Christian, God-fearing, Bible-believing home, and through my own personal experiences, I had plenty of faith. As part of this journey that God had me live, I decided to step into the water. God was my focus. I put my full trust in Him.

Rodger was out of town that Sunday morning for work, and when he returned, I told him I was going back to choir practice on Wednesday night. He thought I was pushing the envelope because he had witnessed the bad days, the sick days, and we both wondered if I would be disabled, breathe properly again, or even if I would live. He was extremely supportive and very protective.

Back to choir practice I went that very next Wednesday night! I stepped into the water, and I can say that God is surely faithful! Ever since that Wednesday night, February 3, 1999, I have been singing praises to God around home, with the congregation, in a choir, praise team, and/or special music! Praise the Lord! God is faithful! **Just trust Me, love God!!**

My medical checkup in April of 1999 showed for the first time in ten years that my white blood count was within normal ranges. At my July 1999 checkup, my doctor chose to not complete more blood work since all blood work was normal in April. She was very amazed at my April and July checkups to see how well I was doing with no symptoms and no medications. I shared a brief version of my testimony with her at my last visit and left with praise and thankfulness in my heart. To this day,

I have had no symptoms of Lupus, and have such an abundance of gratefulness and praise to the Lord Jesus Christ! By faith and belief in His Word, I stepped into the water, and God touched my body. As the Psalmist says, I can sing, and I can praise the Lord with a loud voice. I am very thankful! God is good all the time, and all the time God is good!

Over the course of approximately 15 years, Rodger was involved in several wrecks; none of them were his fault. The one on November 1,1999 especially stands out in our minds. Rodger was sitting at a stoplight behind one vehicle. Before the light changed to green, the driver of a vehicle behind him apparently did not see the red light or was not paying attention. Nonetheless, Rodger was rear-ended with enough force to blow out the back window of his car and break the back of the driver's seat due to the impact of 45 plus miles per hour force while sitting still. Ultimately, this resulted in the total loss of a vehicle purchased three days prior to the accident. I received a call about the wreck at work and rushed to the location. When I arrived, I burst into tears because I took one look at his vehicle and feared the worst. The EMS driver told me he could not believe Rodger got out of the vehicle alive. Rodger was fine, with *no* scratches, cuts or even bruises. It was amazing, and God's grace, mercy, and faithfulness was abundant. Our God is an awesome God!

****

"For I know the plans I have for you," declares the Lord, "plans to prosper you and not to harm you, plans to give you hope and a future." (Jeremiah 29:11).

****

Sometime in the fall of 1997, at the age of 62, Rodger's mother decided to retire due to her declining ability to use computers and the complicated DOS software. We noticed she began showing definitive signs of Alzheimer's around that same time. Over the next seven years, she began a steady state of decline. Rodger's dad began needing help with her and did not want to place her out of the home. Rodger and I had become empty nesters about the same time, so we had already been talking about moving to scale down the size of our home. Together, Rodger and I decided since he was an only child maybe we needed to merge households with his parents so we could help. We were both convinced we could make a difference in their lives for the better. Rodger's parents treated me more like a daughter than a daughter-in-law. They both loved to give, and whenever his mom shopped for their home, we were recipients of many of the same identical items.

We looked for many months for housing options and came close to purchasing a couple of houses other than our final decision. We looked at the house we purchased so many times prior to closing, the builder eventually showed us where the key was located and told us to feel free to go in as often as necessary. After all the looking, we came back to this one house that we had looked at so many times and said, "This is not the one we want." It was just around the corner from where Rodger's parents had lived for about seven years. It was his dad's choice for sure. I had begun to get very weary with all the looking and back and forth to this one house, over and over. One evening, Rodger asked me to go back to that same house and just sit in the driveway and hold hands with him and pray. I was not opposed to praying with him but felt I had looked at the house enough and did not want to go back anymore! I thought, *Okay, one more time*, so off we went again! We prayed, and I guess Rodger thought the praying had changed my heart and I would be willing to look one more time, so in we went for the *50th time*. (Okay, that may be an exaggeration, but it surely felt like the 50th time!) After we had been in the house about five minutes, the doorbell rang. There stood a lady neither of us knew. She wanted to know if we were buying this house. Immediately, I said "no," and Rodger said, "probably not." She inquired why we were moving, and we explained our situation that we were selling our house and his parents' house and moving in together to help take care of his mother. She wanted to know where his parents lived, and we explained around the corner. She wanted to see their house! *Really?!* That was amazing! Rodger told her we did not yet have it on the market, and we had not prepared the inside for showing. She agreed that was fine and asked to just see the yard. Within minutes, we were off around the corner to show the lady the yard. She loved the house from the outside and basically told us she and her husband would buy the house, but she would talk with him first. They purchased the house! The house was not even listed on the real estate market. That was God! We were absolutely amazed at God's provisions and took it as a confirmation that God must have wanted us in the house we were opposed to buying. We merged the two households together in October and November of 2005. The sale of their house was another faith builder, and we are still in that same house. What an amazing journey!

There is no way either of us could have prepared for this change in lifestyle. After several weeks, we realized we were ill prepared for this terrible life-changing debilitating disease of Alzheimer's. Even though Rodger's dad was there as the primary care giver and did an outstanding job taking care of his wife of 50 years, we helped as much as possible. Changing her environment of seven years did not help matters as she became even more confused. We will spare you of the many details. Our hearts were in the right place; however, we were not sure we had made the best decision. Before her Alzheimer's diagnosis, Rodger's mom was so loving and kind.

She laughed just about all the time and loved life every day and loved her family and friends more than words can express. She loved to cook for everyone, and she loved to eat, as well. She loved to shop and would give anyone the shirt off her back. As her disease progressed, Rodger's dad took her to an adult daycare, and after two days, he was told she needed more care than they were equipped to provide. She began in-home Hospice care, and after a few weeks, we realized her health was declining and she needed a higher level of specialized care. In July 2006, we had to move her into a facility to get the help she needed. We were crushed to make this change but could no longer keep her at home. We trusted God that we made a good decision.

After preparing for our marriage ministry, we finally began facilitating Marriage Enrichment classes at our church in September 2006. It was such an awesome feeling. We felt equipped but also very humble. We knew in our hearts we were not perfect people, and we did not have a perfect marriage; however, we knew there are no perfect people in this world, and there are no perfect marriages. We were just two people called by God to do His work and tell as many people about God's plan for marriage as He would allow. We began our very first 11-week class, and with only a few sessions under our belts, Rodger's mother passed on October 11, 2006. Our hearts were broken. At the age of 71, this sweet and precious lady went home to be with the Lord. Holidays are not the same without her, especially Christmas. Christmas was her favorite season, and not a Christmas goes by that we do not think of her love for the holiday and how she decorated very early each year to celebrate this special season of the birth of her Savior, Jesus. In her later stage of Alzheimer's, before we merged households, the decorated Christmas tree was already up in early October because it brought her such happiness. You can only imagine the confused looks on the faces of the children and parents when they rang doorbell to trick-or-treat on Halloween and saw the decorated Christmas tree in her home. To say that we miss her is an understatement, and we miss her enjoying life's journey with us. We look forward to seeing her in Heaven with a perfected body and mind and being able to give her a great big hug!

Rodger's dad continued living with us and felt lost after the death of Mrs. Sauls. After retirement, he worked with a local dealership moving vehicles but stopped work to help with Rodger's mom when her health declined. In April 2007, Mr. Sauls had a stroke, and diabetes made his health matters worse. We were thankful he was living with us as we helped with his recuperation. Over the next year, he made a remarkable recovery and went back living his "normal" life. In October of 2008, Mr. Sauls moved out of our home into a townhome which was about five minutes from us. Up until this point, we had owned the house together and both families shared in the house payment to protect Rodger's dad's equity. For Rodger's dad to have his equity from the house to purchase his townhome, we had to obtain a second mortgage to repay his original investment in the house. At that point, we had 40% more house payment than originally planned, just as the economy and housing market tanked during the "Great Recession."

As untimely as it was, in January 2009, Rodger lost his job of almost 30 years, lacking three months, during a corporate restructuring. He had been with the company since college graduation, and this was a life-changing event. At first, it did not seem real, but as Rodger stayed home sending out applications each day, it became more real. God bless him for handling this disappointing situation so well. That was a time we truly found ourselves leaning heavily on God! Our trust in Him is what helped us make it through such a hard trial. In February 2009, we began facilitating marriage retreats throughout North Carolina. That was our passion, and we would have loved our lay marriage ministry to be full-time but that was not God's plan. The blessing of this circumstance was that since Rodger was out of work at this particular time, he had an opportunity to not only look for another job, but to work on our marriage retreat materials and gather important information to share with couples. God is faithful if we just trust Him, even in the valleys. In March 2009, Rodger was blessed to find another job even though he was not sure it would be permanent. In August 2010, God blessed us to begin facilitating marriage retreats across North Carolina representing the State Baptist Convention in addition to our already scheduled retreats. We felt honored and blessed to have this opportunity. In April 2011, Rodger's job ended, and within a few days, he became a private consultant working from home. His new salary was much less. Lots of questions and feelings came to our minds, but we just needed to trust in the Lord with all our hearts. Though the salary was smaller, we were grateful for Rodger's new work opportunity as part of our adventure through life together.

****

After seeking counseling with several trained and degreed Godly men and women, much soul searching, and much prayer and trust in God, our oldest daughter, Heather, remarried in April 2009. As she describes it, "I married my complete match in every way!" She and her husband, Andy, are extremely happy, and we give God all the praise and glory for this mountaintop experience. He is a Southern Baptist pastor in Faison, North Carolina and is an attentive husband and awesome Dad.

****

"The Lord bless you and keep you; the Lord make his face shine upon you and be gracious to you; the Lord turn His face toward you and give you peace." (Numbers 6: 24-26).

****

Another big family adventure began in 2011 when our family grew a little bigger. On July 18, 2011, our first grandbaby was born, a huge nine-pound handsome boy. Oh, what a blessing! There were no words to describe our feelings and emotions as first-time grandparents! However, Heather was sick during his birth, and we were told with her complications due to preeclampsia, her kidneys were shutting down, she was swelling, and she could die and even the baby as well. We all joined hands around her hospital bed and prayed fervently! With much prayer and faith, she was fine and so was our sweet grandson! Once again, God was faithful as we placed our trust in Him.

Life progressed somewhat normal for a while, but another trial was around the corner. As a result of complications with his kidneys, stroke, diabetes and being a burn victim, Rodger's dad developed gangrene in July 2013 and was sent to the hospital. He was in and out of the hospital and nursing facility due to complications. On October 7, 2013, Rodger's dad met Jesus face to face while in the hospital with Rodger by his side, and he no longer faces the complications of burns and diabetes. Our hearts, once again, were broken. It did not seem that he should be gone at 78 years old, but there were too many health issues working against him. We went through such a roller coaster of emotions and thought processes. He had always seemed to have such a will to live and passion for life. This man loved watching races, football, and eating out with everyone. He loved to trade cars and buy boats. He loved to give and watch people receive gifts that he had meticulously purchased. He loved his family! He was now reunited with Mrs. Sauls, (aka Grandma Trina). We look forward to watching races together with him in heaven one day.

During that same time, Rodger's contracts with work slowed to a minimum. He had little income, and it was so easy to question God and ask why. We had so many questions in our minds. *Do we go to plan B or plan C? Do we use what we have saved for retirement?* While we questioned in that period of great anxiety, God whispered, "Just trust me." However, we had other questions about Rodger's job, my ability to retire, help my parents, help with the new grandbaby, and devote more time to marriage ministry. The questions kept coming. *Why are we experiencing so much pain? Why can we not facilitate more retreats per year, and why is there not more interest?* God continued to say the same thing, "Just trust me." We continued being faithful to the Lord and trusting in Him. We must trust God when we cannot see the way.

****

"Have I not commanded you? Be strong and courageous. Do not be terrified; do not be discouraged, for the Lord your God will be with you wherever you go." (Joshua 1:9).

****

In December 2013, we received news that our oldest daughter was having another baby in August 2014! That was another mountaintop experience that made us happy. However, in March of 2014, she began having thyroid problems during her pregnancy. We praised God that her appointment showed the baby was fine and her hyperthyroidism was a mild form, determined to be due to pregnancy. She had a nodule on the left side of her thyroid, but the biopsy showed no cancer. Her levels were also normal. *God, You, are so good!*

I realized, after discussing retirement with my work Human Resources Department, I could retire October 2014 with 32 years without much difference in my paycheck. Therefore, after much prayer, I retired to help my parents, as my mom was progressing with Alzheimer, and my dad had problems with heart disease and needed help. My oldest brother had retired and began helping with our parents' banking needs, medication errands, and taking them grocery shopping. Shortly after my retirement, my dad was diagnosed with Parkinson Disease in January 2015, and that was an extremely sad time for all of us as he was very dedicated to my mom and her needs. If that was not enough, in June 2015, my oldest brother, who was helping with our parents, died of cardiac arrest at the age of 64. What a shock! This felt like a bad dream! **Just trust Me, love God.** When I arrived at the hospital after my sister-in-law called about his passing, they ushered me to where they were holding his body for family to arrive. I went into the room by his side and quietly prayed if it be God's will for him to be raised to life just like Lazarus, the widow's son, the Shunammite woman's son, and the resurrection of Christ! As I paused for a while and turned around, one of the nurses leaned over and whispered in my ear, "Your faith has touched my heart." Linwood was such a good big brother and is missed by all of us. He and I enjoyed some special conversations about six weeks prior to his death. Afterwards, these conversations felt to be ordained specifically by God not knowing his death was imminent. I began doing the things my brother had done for our parents after his passing. My brother's death was another terrible blow to my dad after just being diagnosed with Parkinson because he grieved his son's loss every day. My mom became progressively worse; however, my dad was very committed to keeping her at home and taking care of her with my help. I could see his health declining but had no idea what was coming so soon.

Thursday, April 28, 2016 was my routine day to clean my parents' house, bring weekly food, do laundry, and do personal care for Mom. Dad was feeling exceptionally weak and tired. I returned on Friday to find the same. On Saturday, Rodger went with me, and we tried to get Dad to go to the hospital, but he decided to move up his upcoming doctor's appointment from Wednesday to Monday instead of going to the emergency room that day. We decided to check in on them again the next day,

Sunday, and we informed him we would be there early. I was anxious to get Sunday behind me and get him to the doctor on Monday morning. His mind was fixated on going to the doctor as opposed to the hospital. That Saturday evening, I went to bed exhausted and wondering just how sick Dad really was at that point. On Sunday morning, May 1, 2016, I awakened early, and very clearly felt my dad had passed. I looked at my bedside clock and it was 5:01 am, and it hit me, it was also 5-1, May 1, 2016. I got up, got dressed, and found the folder with all Dad and Mom's funeral information. Rodger had already determined he would go with me to check on them again that day. He asked me what I was doing with the folder, and I told him that God whispered to my heart, and I believed Dad was gone. What a 50-minute drive that was for me! God's voice seemed to say, "Janet, trust me; my timing is perfect." But my heart was broken as I cried with the feeling he was gone. When God tells you, you believe it for sure, but did I misunderstand? No, I knew in my heart, God was right. I called and called their telephone, but no answer. Mom's Alzheimer's mind had progressed to the point she almost never answered the telephone. I called for 50 minutes during the long drive home. When we arrived, the doors were locked. It took a while, but Mom came to the door. She looked oblivious to where she was, and I could tell something was wrong by the looks of the house. I ran as fast as my feet would take me through the house. There he was, his physical body on the bedroom floor, but his soul was with our Lord Jesus Christ. *Lord, your voice to me was right!* It was so painful that I cried like someone was ripping me apart, but I remembered that Daddy always told us growing up, "Do not cry for me when I'm gone because I will be in Heaven." *Okay, Daddy, but my heart is broken to pieces and I cannot stop crying.* Mom was in the den with Rodger so unaware of what was happening, or was she? You see, Dad had those license plates we talked about in an earlier chapter in this book in boxes in his study. Mom had found the license plates and used them to decorate their bedroom all around his body. It was the most touching and amazing thing I had ever seen. As I went back to the den, I was crying uncontrollably, and Mom looked at me and said, "Janet, don't cry like that, you're too pretty to cry." Okay, so I cried harder and harder. Could there possibly be any more tears? Oh yes!

There were so many calls to make with so many people to contact: rescue, Sheriff's Department, and the funeral home. Then my mind shifted to my Mama! What were we going to do about Mama!!?? She needed 24/7 care! *God, we trust you, but this is awful. This is gut wrenching! God help us!* As the emergency personnel arrived and were talking with us, I gave each one a 70-TIMES-7 license plate explaining to them that they needed to forgive people: the John Doe citizen who was disrespectful, the boss who just did not understand, the neighbor who was rude, the co-workers who got on their last nerve, their wife who may not respect them or understand them, and most of all ask forgiveness from God on a daily basis, the one who died on the cross for all of us! One of the officers looked over at me with tears in his eyes and could hardly speak but said, "we've never been to a house like this, never been on a call like this." His reaction made my heart happy because I could only imagine how passionate I had been with them up to that point. Daddy loved 70-TIMES-7 and the meaning of the license plate. He wanted everyone to know about God's forgiveness. Two days later, May 3, 2016, we hired some ladies in the community to stay with Mom around the clock so we could take care of funeral details. Mom fell early that morning getting out of bed. We took her to the Emergency Room and were told she had broken all her ribs on the right side. She was in serious pain, and the Emergency Room visit did nothing to help calm her mind that was already very confused. The next day, May 4, 2016, was Daddy's funeral and burial. In my traumatic mental state, when I arrived at the funeral that afternoon, I was very emotional and upset. It is always very calming to remember that God is always with us.

****

"In the same way, the Spirit helps us in our weakness. We do not know what we ought to pray for, but the Spirit himself intercedes for us with groans that words cannot express." (Romans 8:26).

****

The Bible tells us in 1 Thessalonians 4:13 to not grieve without hope because Jesus has risen from the dead and gives hope to all who believe in Him that we will rise with Him. Even though we go through a deep valley at the time of a loved one's death, we can all still have hope.

Immediately after the burial, while still at the cemetery, I received a phone call that Mom was sick, and we needed to return to her home immediately. She was taken to the hospital, and we were told she had a severe UTI and would probably not live! *WHAT!? NO!* My tears flowed! I cried out to God for comfort and peace! *What is going on? Lord, please help us! I just lost my daddy. How can I be losing my mama, too?!* This was not real. Again, it seemed that God said to my spirit, "Just trust me Janet." *How? This is too much! God, why?*

Mom stayed in the hospital until Friday, May 6, 2016, and we realized we faced another dilemma. We did not have a Power of Attorney to help Mom with the care she needed. We could not imagine how we would obtain one due to Mom's mental condition and her physical sickness. How would she ever answer any attorney's questions? Mom was to be discharged from the hospital and placed in an Assisted Living/Memory Care facility. When I arrived at the hospital on the 6th, Mom seemed so clear in her mind; it took me by surprise. A hospital chaplain came in to visit with Mom, and she knew that she had four children and one of them had died, she knew her name, birth date, and other pertinent information. We were blown away! My sister called her husband to have the attorney come to the hospital so we could try to get the Power of Attorney, and guess what? We did! The chaplain confirmed with the attorney that Mom had mentally clarity, and he had a good conversation with her. God knew we needed this Power of Attorney to properly take care of Mom, and as usual, His timing was perfect! **Just trust Me, love God!** A short time later, Mom left the hospital via emergency vehicle with me in tow headed to her new home the memory care facility. She was very scared as we got settled inside the vehicle. Mom was strapped in on a gurney, and I was across the aisle from her buckled in a seat. We had a 45-minute drive to the facility. The vehicle was very loud and shook badly. I had never been in an emergency vehicle, so I did not know what was or was not normal. Honestly, at that point, I was a bit rattled with everything that had happened in my life and what I was dealing with currently. I began to chat with the young man who was logging information into the computer and offered him a 70-TIMES-7 license plate. (Yes, I continued by Dad's legacy to share about forgiveness.) We had a wonderful discussion as he shared that was a very timely gift with his current marriage situation. The roaring and shaking of the vehicle became so bad, I loudly asked the young girl driving if she could slow down a bit because Mom was frightened and crying uncontrollably. By that time, I had unbelted and laid myself across her body singing in her ear to calm her anxiety. The young girl slowed down, but it did not help Mom. About 30 seconds after the driver slowed the vehicle, we experienced a tire blow out! Initially, I did not know what had happened as there was a very loud bang, and the vehicle was off the road in one second! When the dust settled, it was like a quick dream, but we were alive to tell about this event. The young girl asked me if I knew how close we were to falling over the embankment. She did not have to tell me. YES, we missed it by one or two feet! She also shared that just six weeks prior to this day, she had received training through a fire department how to maneuver an emergency vehicle during a tire blow out. That is not all! She stated that she was not supposed to have been the one driving the vehicle that day, but at the last minute, she became the driver. Anyone want to guess who was with us that day?! Praise the Lord, God Himself! The angels were all around us. One other interesting point is that when the vehicle came to rest on the shoulder of the road, a nice and helpful law enforcement officer was right behind us! He stopped and directed traffic so she could get the vehicle away from the embankment, back on the road, and drive down a dirt path to wait for another emergency vehicle to pick us up! Let me pause right now and thank the Lord for his goodness, mercy, grace, and protection! Unfortunately, because I unbelted to help Mom, I fractured my foot when we wrecked.

After about 45 minutes, we switched vehicles and headed to Mom's new home. That day was Mom and Dad's 66th Anniversary. My heart was so grateful for our protection, but I was in a daze. So much had happened. My thoughts were jumbled, but God continued being faithful. I was feeling the effects of prayers since Dad had passed which had been only five days. I did not want to place Mom anywhere, but for many reasons, this was the best decision. After being on the road about 10 minutes, we had a car almost hit our vehicle in the side; a near miss. *Lord, you are so faithful.*

Each day of this journey, I visited Mom as she plummeted down with this terrible disease with her crying, confusion, agitation, swelling legs from congestive heart failure, and poor functioning kidneys. How sad. Why?! I just lost my dad. I did not feel that I had any tears left. I was not ready to lose my mom. I needed to trust God and not worry. These song lyrics came to my mind, "Lord, I Need You, Oh, I Need You, Every Hour I Need You."

On May 10, 2016, as I was returning from an appointment and was on my way to check on Mom, I called Rodger to chat. Unknowing to me, he had been to Urgent Care with what appeared to be a kidney stone and did not want to call me to add worry and upset to my already full and sad plate. On May 12, he went to the Emergency Room due to more kidney stone symptoms and low-grade fever. On the 13th, he had an appointment with a urologist who suggested he wait through the weekend to see if could pass stone. By the 16th, Rodger had not passed the stone, and they scheduled him for surgery. On May 18, Rodger had outpatient surgery at the hospital to remove the stone and was sent home. By the way, when we talked with Rodger's surgeon prior to leaving the hospital, we gave him a 70-TIMES-7 license plate and discussed forgiveness. Rodger consumed 64 ounces of fluid at the hospital, and within two hours of getting home, he realized he could not urinate and was having extreme pain. We made an emergency trip back to the urologist's office. On the way, I was extremely upset and driving as quickly as possible still trying to be safe. Hindsight is always 20/20, so in retrospect, I probably should have called an emergency vehicle to take us. As I looked over at Rodger in the car, he was beginning to turn a very grey ashy color! I knew he must be overly sick, and I could hardly focus on driving. There was so much going on in our lives at this one moment. I was sobbing and told Rodger, "If this is what happens in your life when you are serving in marriage ministry, then I'm done, I'm done. Do you hear me? DONE! No more marriage ministry and no more giving license plates!" We will come back to those statements in a moment. We rushed into the doctor's office, and when they took one look at Rodger he was rushed to the back. They inserted a catheter and removed 51 ounces of fluid from his bladder. A typical bladder holds approximately 16 ounces of fluid. This explains why he looked like death!

Just minutes earlier, I had exclaimed to Rodger that we needed to be done with our ministry. As the nurse administered care to him, the first thing out of my mouth was, "Please help him; I love this man. We have been married 40 years, and I cannot think about anything happening to him!" The opportunity to share Jesus occurred in the presence of a nurse that day. In minutes, were back to a marriage ministry opportunity with this nurse which ensued a conversation about marriage. Then we discussed the 70-TIMES-7 license plate and forgiveness. To our surprise, she already knew about the license plate. Rodger's surgeon had shared about his license plate at staff meeting earlier on the morning of surgery. She told us she was sorry about Rodger's experience but so grateful we had been able to share with her about marriage and forgiveness. God is good, and His timing is always perfect! My emotions from exhaustion and love for my husband in his time of dire sickness skewed my mind for a moment but I quickly retrieved my heart back to God's calling on our lives and His purpose and plans for us. **Just trust me, love God**. We felt God's presence from the prayers of the saints! That is the only way we make sense of life in times like this. It is through faith in Jesus Christ and trust in His ability to give us peace and strength! God is faithful! The doctor's office sent Rodger home with the catheter, and we thought all was well. We were so glad to have this saga over and done. Or so we thought...

On May 19, because of ongoing complications, we made a visit to the Emergency Room again. They removed the initial catheter and replaced it with, as Rodger likes to say, "a garden hose variety". Then, the medical team discovered a large blood clot in the bladder which was causing his complications. It required a process known as bladder irrigation where multiple liters of fluid were flushed through his bladder each hour. He was then admitted to the hospital and stayed three days and two nights. This was Rodger's first hospital experience as a patient. God was with us each day. During this time, Mom was not doing well, so I spent each night with Rodger at the hospital and waited for our sweet helpful daughters to relieve me each morning. When they arrived, I went home to freshen up, went to see Mom and then went back to the hospital to repeat the routine. Both of us most definitely felt God's presence with us and knew He was the sustaining grace. We were so appreciative of all the prayers from everyone. Each day, I wondered what was next. Would this be over soon? Why were we experiencing these difficulties? Was it for God's glory? Well, yes, if we shared about God's faithfulness and our continued trust in Him. It was so hard losing my dad, seeing my mom suffer with Alzheimer's, and watching my husband I love so much go through this event. Some readers may think our trials pale in comparison to the life events they have experienced or what real pain and suffering in life is about. While we do not know what others have experienced, we do know that God is there for all who are suffering, feeling sad, feeling fearful, experiencing hopelessness, grieving, and for those who are going through daily routines without knowing Him. We need to be faithful, trust Him, and ask for His help. He is always there! The more we go through, and the more we trust Him, the

more faith we receive. These experiences are faith builders for us.

As Mom's caregiver, I felt it was time to move her
from the facility she had been living in for approximately
six weeks. The new facility was three times further from
my home; however, the move needed to happen. I was
scheduled to move her on the Friday before June 20, but
paperwork was not available until the 20th which was my
60th birthday! It was hard. I felt sick inside with so much
going on. *Lord, I need to trust you more than ever. Help
me! Give me strength! Thank You Lord!* There is a song
that comes to my mind when I think about this. That song
tells us to thank the Lord for making us whole because
his salvation is great and free. I could not have made any
sense of these days without Jesus Christ and His grace
and mercy, peace, and comfort.

Each visit with Mom was different as she had
good days and not so good days. Some days she had
mental clarity, and was happy, and quiet. Some days she
had crying, agitation, swelling legs, and UTI's. Overall,
Mom was now in a good facility. With that said, the people who worked there are like all of us, not perfect peo-

ple so that makes for a non-perfect place. There were challenges, but there are challenges in any situation with an Alzheimer's patient. In January 2017, we were told Mom's condition had deteriorated, and she was probably in her final phase of Alzheimer's. They also told us she possibly had only a few weeks or months to live because of her congestive heart failure and poor kidney function. Several days later, Mom became better and seemed to have life left. As her doctor and nurse stated, "Only God knows her timing." Over the next several months, Mom began not wanting to sleep at night but sleeping more during the day and not eating well some days. There were some hard days watching Mom decline. I cried many days after being with her. My heart was broken. It became difficult for her to stay awake and hold her head up for me to shampoo cap wash, dry, and roll her hair. She was basically not coherent; however, we enjoyed listening to her Gaither CD together each week during her hair time, and sometimes she sang along with me. It was precious! Mom also had many days when she was alert, would talk with the ladies where she stayed, and communicated with me about different things from her past. God continued to give me strength; however, one day when I left, I cried out and asked God to take Mom to Heaven to be with my brother, and my dad. After that outburst, I felt that maybe I just needed to pray the model prayer in God's Word, Matthew 6:10 "Your will be done." That is exactly what Rodger and I continued praying. August 24, 2017 was such an amazing day! When I arrived to see Mom, she was alert, bright eyed, with clarity of mind, and gave me the biggest hug I had received from her in years! I ran back to the closet in her room and grabbed my camera from my purse and took several photos of Mom. The next three weeks were some of the sweetest and best weeks I had experienced with her. Those weeks gave me precious memories. Several chain of events, four to be exact, happened on September 14, 2017 that caused me to tell Rodger, "God is up to something to-day." It was all so powerful that I wrote each event on the calendar. One of those happenings was randomly hear-ing my dad's funeral song that reminded us that we can face tomorrow, because Jesus lives. I did not necessarily know these events had anything to do with Mom, but I knew God was working. On that same day, when I went to visit Mom after church, she looked very pale. I thought maybe because I had not yet put on her makeup. She did not eat very much and was very sleepy. This was not really all that unusual because she had been through similar phases. I left, went home, and then to church for several functions. Later that evening, the facility called to let me know Mom was unresponsive and had been taken to the hospital. She was peaceful and calm, with no crying, no agitation, and no pain. The doctors suggested 24 to 48 hours, but I had heard similar reports before. They did state that only God knew for sure her time.

On September 18th around 8:15 PM, I got in bed to try and rest for the night as I was mentally, physically, and emotionally exhausted. My mind was racing around thinking of all the upcoming plans going on within the coming week. Would I follow through, stay with Mom, would it be a day, a week, a month, or would it be like back in January with many months to follow? I was restless, so I prayed and asked God to calm my mind. I felt in my heart Mom would pass on 9-19, the next day. I immediately looked at the clock and it was 9:19 PM. If you remember, when my dad passed, I felt God stir in my heart as well. That is why I looked to see the time.

I awoke on the 19th at 5:30 AM to get an early start to spend the day with Mom since I felt this was her last day. I left home at 6:31 AM and shortly received a call that she passed at 6:31 AM. I arrived at the facility at 6:50 and missed her passing by 19 minutes on the 19th. My heart was broken, but she was with Jesus, my dad, my brother, and her parents. God was merciful. But I missed her. I was thankful she was no longer in an Alzheimer's mind and that she was perfected, but she was my mama. She was so sweet. Now with both my parents and a brother in heaven, I realized more than ever that I need to trust God's perfect timing. *I need to trust you with everything, God. Please give me strength.* As anyone who has lost an elderly sick parent can attest, this is a natural progression of life, and we feel thankful they are no longer sick or in pain. Even when it is a Dad, a Mom, or a brother… We grieve. We mourn. It is surreal. It is part of life's journey.

Over the last 44 years of marriage, kids, grandkids, parents, church, and careers, I feel that Rodger has done an outstanding job of prioritizing God, home, church, and work. While being caregivers for his dad and mom and my dad and mom, we tried to maintain the same balance in our lives and marriage. It is so difficult for most women to clear their minds during any given day. As most probably know, women's brains stay on fire most of the time. Mine is no different. Praise God for an understanding, loving, and supportive husband who helped me as much with my parents as I did with his during their times of sickness and death. *Thank you, God that we were able to help each other and share with each other through times of sadness and times of happiness by trusting in YOU!!*

Study and Reflection

- Think about a mountaintop experience you have encountered. Think about a time when you went through a valley. In which experience could you see God at work? In which experience did you feel closer to God? If you are married, did you draw closer to your spouse on the mountaintop or in the valley?

- If you are married or engaged, pause for a moment to think back when you first met. Think about how you displayed your best for those special dates. Think about the fun things you did together, the places you went together, and how excited you were to be together. More than likely, you put a lot of time and energy into pursuing each other. Now ask yourself; do we still put forth our best for each other, do we still do fun things together, and finally do we still date. If the answer is yes to all of these, great! You probably have or will have a happy and healthy marriage. If the answer is no, why not? Ask yourself if he or she is any less important than when you first dated? What changes do you need to make to begin pursuing each other again? When we stop pursuing, if we are not careful, we may find that they have wandered away physically, or emotionally.

- It is easy to pursue God when things are going well in life. Do you pursue and trust Him when things appear hopeless or dark? If so, how does He respond? Does He say, not now, I am too busy, or does He does greet you with outstretched arms of His love, grace, mercy, and peace?

- Reflect on a time when God was there for you and you felt his presence during a difficult or tragic situation.

- If we do not communicate with someone on a regular basis, it is most often hard to have a close personal relationship with them. Do you prioritize God first in your life and set aside time to read His Word, pray and talk with Him daily? Do you give Him your best or what you have left over at the end of the day? Even if you have had a long personal relationship with the Lord, it is always appropriate to pause and ask; Lord, am I living my life in a way that is pleasing to you, and if not, give me the desire, determination, and strength to do so every day according to your will for my life.

- It is important that we always try to praise God in the valleys as well as the mountaintop experiences. Have there been times you wanted to blame God instead of praising him? He is always faithful to give us his love, comfort, and His sustaining grace.

- Have there been times in your life when you wanted to blame others for your poor decisions or actions? Always remember your relationship with Jesus is very personal, and we will all stand before Jesus one day to give an account for ourselves and not others regardless of their actions. Remember, they will give account for their own life.

CHAPTER 5

There Is No Perfect Time to Do What God Has Asked You to Do

We spoke about my nudge from God to write this book early in 2014, and Rodger agreed that we needed to follow through with this book. We both had a passion to write and put on paper in a short time a good portion of the book. However, there were immediate family member deaths in 2015, 2016, and 2017. There seemed to be no time to write, and grief emotions were high. In October 2017, we tried to find time to write and complete the book, but again, busyness seemed to prevail, and we did not make this happen. We often talked about the need to get busy doing what we knew God has urged my heart to do but life continued to happen, and there never seemed to be enough time. My home workstation was not ergonomic enough, there was housework that needed to be done, I enjoyed keeping our grandsons, our marriage ministry was thriving and a priority, and Rodger was still working full-time. We convinced ourselves that we were tired and needed to rest, that there were not enough hours in the day, or we wrestled with what format to use. We asked ourselves, "Can this be done in Microsoft Word or do we need new software, and who would publish our book?" "What if our book was not enough pages to encourage a publisher to accept our work?" The list went on and on, as did the days, weeks, months, and years.

During the Covid-19 global pandemic, we were online for church each Sunday morning, and we also watched services from various churches during the week. On Sunday, August 9, 2020, we watched three different services with the last sermon entitled "Tick Tock Goes the Clock" presented by Pastor Brian Frost at Providence Baptist Church, Raleigh, North Carolina. I will share with you some of the prominent things that Pastor Frost said that stirred our hearts.

Pastor Frost explained that we have a part of God's mission that will last forever. The sermon scriptures were found in Ecclesiastes 11:1–12:8. We have fears, anxieties, and sin. God's grace helps us be courageous with promises to never leave us or forsake us.

He cuts us with His Word, but as soon as He does, He heals and mends us. In Ecclesiastes, Solomon urges us to dream, and risk, and run. He used an illustration of farming wheat to play it safe in life or risk everything to take a calculated risk or chase a dream. Sometimes bad things happen but we should be hopeful enough to risk. Pastor Frost asked the questions, "What is something you believe God has asked you to do that you have not done? What is a dream God has put upon your heart and you think, 'well one day,' but you have not pursued that dream?" At that moment, I looked over at Rodger with a surprised look and smile on my face and said, "Okay, we need to finish our book!" Pastor Frost said we try to wait until the perfect time; we want to know the answers to everything. If we have breath in our lungs, today is the day to dream, risk, and run so let's do that right now.

Life is unpredictable. Sometimes rain falls on you and other times it does not. Sometimes trees fall to the north and sometimes to the south. If we are waiting for the perfect set up when everything is perfect, we will never sow a seed, and we will never reap a dream. Quit making excuses for not doing what God told you to do, you never know what will happen. Trust God. Life is mysterious. We try to know everything about a situation before we try to do what we need to do. The Bible tell us we will not always know everything we want to know. He said that some would say, I would start my book, but I do not know if it will get published. I promise you, the book you never write will never get published. Write the first paragraph; you never know where it will lead.

****

"Whoever watches the wind will not plant; whoever looks at the clouds will not reap. As you do not know the path of the wind, or how the body is formed in a mother's womb, so you cannot understand the work of God, the Maker of all things." (Ecclesiastes 11:4-5).

****

At this point, I was up on my feet looking straight at the television with my mouth standing open in amazement. Rodger, I exclaimed, "Did he just specifically mention writing a book?" Rodger was chuckling at me because he was as astonished as I was at that moment! We had a renewed zeal to complete this book! This was not coincidental, and God again was urging. It is time to ask: What has God called us to do that we have not done yet?

On Monday morning, August 10 (our youngest daughter's birthday), I began working on the book feverishly for six hours, seven hours on Tuesday, and the same on Wednesday. We did not know the answers to any of our questions, but what we did know is that by God's strength and help, we would complete this book and make every attempt to have it published. I will be honest, my neck, shoulders, and back were not happy without all the comforts of ergonomic fluffs, and our house did not feel as spiffy clean as usual, but by the grace of God and strength only He can give, we were determined to complete the task for His glory and His purpose. When we feel small, He gives us huge support, and in our weakness He is strong. There is an old song that some may remember from Kittie Suffield, and some of the lyrics are, "Little is much when God is in it, labor not for wealth or fame," and that sums up us and our book. Again, we were trusting in God to help us complete this book is for His glory and no other purpose as small as it may seem.

Study and Reflection

- Has God laid something on your heart or nudged you to do something that you have tried to ignore or refused to do?

- What is preventing you from doing the task God has asked you to do? Is it because you are afraid, too busy, or you feel unequipped?

- There may be obstacles in your life, like busyness keeping you from moving forward with His will for your life. What changes do you need to make, and are you willing to make changes even if it means sacrifice?

- Have you asked God for the strength and courage to take a step of faith?

CHAPTER 6

The Unexpected

After diligently working to complete our book over the last several days as opposed to allowing life to get in the way as we had done for the last six years, today, August 12, 2020, we heard the unexpected. This past April 2020, I noticed a dark area in the bottom cup of Rodger's ear. We did not really think much about it at first, and then it began looking sort of angry, began growing, and had some drainage, so we became a bit more concerned. Rodger's dermatologist's office was closed due to the Pandemic, and when it opened, we were not thrilled about being in a doctor's office. On August 5, Rodger had a biopsy at the dermatologist's office and received the dreaded call today. Rodger was diagnosed with melanoma in his left ear. We were both shocked, stunned, and certainly did not expect that news. A growth maybe, a cyst or a cancer to be removed, but not melanoma. He was scheduled to be seen by a UNC Chapel Hill doctor on August 17 because his dermatologist told him this was extremely rare, and she did not deal with this type cancer in the ear and knew it required plastic surgery. *Lord, we come before you right now on behalf of Rodger's ear and the diagnosis. We trust you with our hearts, minds, and souls. We believe in healing and believe this will not be a bad situation. You have power over us, every situation we have faced before, and this situation, too; you can heal, in Jesus' Name!*

Shortly after I typed the above paragraph, I was headed to pick up and deliver food to a neighboring family. At the last minute, I wanted to attach a get-well card but did not have any on hand. I found several professionally printed Christian note cards with scriptures I had been given from our youngest daughter for my birthday and had several left, so I read through them to find just the right verse for my friend. There it was, just the perfect one. The words were from the psalmist, "He will not let your foot slip-he who watches over you will not slumber" (Psalm 121:3). My OCD prompted me to ensure the verse matched the scripture, so I reached for my Bible that was already right there beside my computer to check

Psalm 121:3. To my surprise, my Bible was open to that exact chapter on the right side page. I had forgotten at the time, but a few days earlier while working on the book, I had looked up another passage in Psalm that was on the same page. In the margin next to Psalm 121, I had written, "God our helper, wants to move the mountain; do not lose hope, focus on God's promises. Our help comes from God; He will never leave us or forsake us. Folks, I was in tears at this moment and called both of our daughters on the way out the door to tell them God is up to something, and I am trusting in Him. Some reading these lines will say I am weird, and all of this is merely coincidence, but I will say this was God's providence! The number 121 has been a special number in our family for many years, and God has used that number on multiple occasions, to give encouragement and confirmation to our hearts. He has used the number 121 to show His faithfulness, sovereignty, and healing powers through a wedding venue address, hospital room number, first home address, job change, and even a restaurant address! To think God was that detail-oriented in dealing with us this day when we needed strength and encouragement was extremely overwhelming and humbling! *We love you Lord! We worship you in Spirit and Truth!*

Today, August 17, I awakened for Rodger's appointment anxious, sad, and weary, and tried to pray but felt distracted. Rodger was quiet as we drove along to see the Chapel Hill Oncologist for a consultation. On the way there, I prayed and asked God to give us peace, strength, and comfort.

****

"He will have no fear of bad news; his heart is steadfast, trusting in the Lord." (Psalm 112:7).

****

The oncologist surgeon was great! He stated it appeared the melanoma was in earliest stages but could only be confirmed after surgery. He also completed a total body check for additional melanoma and found none. If he finds no melanoma present in any lymph nodes during surgery, it will be considered stage 2. If melanoma is present in one or more lymph nodes, it will be considered stage 3, and he believes the chances are 25 percent of being found in lymph nodes. Because the melanoma is in the bottom cup of the ear, it will be extremely difficult to remove and get clear margins, so they may have to remove some cartilage which could require grafting and reconstructive surgery to the lower portion of the ear. He said surgery will probably take three hours. It was late afternoon, and we were very tired and drained. It was an emotional day full of uncertainties and the unknown, but God is all knowing and has this in His hands. Again, He says, **"Just trust Me, love God."**

The next day, I spent most of the morning making about 40 small red crosses out of some red velvet ribbon I had left over from Christmas wreath bows. I placed each one strategically over doorways of coming and going and areas Rodger touches and stays around most days as he works from home. I placed the red crosses on windows, lamps, cabinets, over bathroom mirrors, the bed, and the kitchen island chair he sits in each day. We prayed fervently for Rodger!

****

"The blood will be a sign for you on the houses where you are; and when I see the blood, I will pass over you. No destructive plague will touch you when I strike Egypt." (Exodus 12:13).

****

****

"But he was pierced for our transgressions, he was crushed for our iniquities; the punishment that brought us peace was upon him, and by his wounds we are healed." (Isaiah 53:5).

****

We spent the last several days in much prayer, praise and worship, and thanksgiving for blessings. My heart was so heavy, and I cried out to God to heal Rodger's ear and spare him this pain and suffering. Rodger said to me several times, "I am no better than anyone else to go through this situation or cancer." However, I know God is more than able to heal his ear in the name of Jesus!

****

"Great are the works of the Lord; they are pondered by all who delight in them. Glorious and majestic are his deeds, and his righteousness endures forever." (Psalm 111:2-3).

****

We need to think about all God has done for us and give Him thanks! Rodger read to me an article in the news on August 24, 2020, about a 20-year old woman in Detroit who paramedics performed CPR and other life-reviving methods for 30 minutes but pronounced her dead August 23. Hours later, workers at a funeral home discovered she was still breathing before they embalmed her body. I declared to Rodger by faith in Jesus I will not believe any news about his health other than good news, and my faith will take me right up to the funeral home!

On August 26, we saw the plastic surgeon who was wonderful and informative. He told us that he would not know exactly the extent of Rodger's surgery reconstruction or size of the graft site until after the surgeon removed the melanoma. He would then determine how deep he would need to go to repair the ear and how much cartilage, if any, was removed. He also made sure we understood that due to the skin graft the first 24 to 48 hours would be critical and Rodger might have to stay overnight at the hospital. At that point, since I had been allowed to be present for the oncology surgeon and plastic surgeon office appointments, I was hoping I would be allowed to stay with Rodger if he had to spend a night in the hospital after surgery. With Covid-19 regulations, many hospitals did not let family members stay. I moved ahead in faith. I packed a pull bag and my backpack as if we would stay for one night and had plenty to eat and drink. Also, as mentioned in an earlier chapter, my dad's

70-TIMES-7 (forgiveness) license plate has always had a special place in our lives, and this day would be no different. Therefore, I packed 15 of the plates in my pull bag. I would know who to give them to at the right time.

I awakened on August 27, at 5:20 AM to prepare for Rodger's surgery day. We arrived at UNC Chapel Hill Hospital at 9:20 AM for a 10:00 AM Lymphoscintigram in which they injected dye in Rodger's ear to determine the location of any nearby lymph nodes. If the dye traveled to any lymph nodes, the surgeon would remove and biopsy any of those nodes during surgery which was scheduled to follow the Lymphoscintigram. The medical team took Rodger back for the test at 10:15 AM, and I found a seat in a crowded waiting room. I sat there quietly—praying, thinking, reading my dad's scriptures he had given me when I was sick with Lupus—and felt sort of numb. God was with me, and I knew people were praying because I felt His calming presence. I looked around the room to see who I needed to give a license plate to, and there were so many people, I knew I had not packed enough for everyone, nor did I feel the time was right. After Rodger's test was complete at 11:15 AM, we were taken to the Operating Room waiting room to wait for surgery. We were told surgery would be at approximately 1:00 PM.

As I walked into the room, I felt my heart beat a little faster, so I took a few deep breaths. Rodger was such a trooper but was exhausted because he had not slept well for a few weeks. He is a left side sleeper, and the left ear did not like his weight on the melanoma. He rolled around a lot to try to find a good position to rest. The night prior to surgery, of course, was no different. As we arrived at the waiting room, I scanned around the area and noticed many people. As I prayed and thought about who I would give the license plate to, I saw a lady who worked there, and I felt she was the one I should approach. I stepped up to just behind the Covid-19 social distance line and tried to follow all rules. I told her,

> "I have a little gift for you today. Thanks for
> being so helpful as my husband has surgery.
> We appreciate you. This is a license plate my
> dad had made in 1993. It is a similar repli-
> ca of his own personal license plate, and
> he purchased sheets of aluminum and had
> someone make them in Wilson, North Caro-
> lina. He was a minister and used the plates in

his ministry. We use them in our lay marriage ministry that Rodger was called to by God in 2004. The 70-TIMES-7 means forgiveness. Forgiveness between us and God, forgiving others even if they do not ask and forgiving ourselves."

The worker burst into tears and hugged the license plate. She told me that was just for her. My heart was so touched that I had tears in my eyes and was overwhelmed with emotion. We continued to sit and wait and watch the clock. I asked every hour about the schedule and when Rodger might be called to be prepped for surgery. The 1:00 PM surgery time changed to 2:00 PM...and 2:00 PM changed to 3:00 PM. Around 2:30 PM, workers saw how tired Rodger was when she saw him napping in the chair, and one asked if he would like them to find a bed for him to rest while we waited. He kindly declined. We felt welcomed and well-taken care of that day. Finally, at 3:09 PM, we were escorted to the prep area of the Operation Room! What a relief to finally be on the way to surgery. However, our hearts were broken for another family when we realized that the reason we had to wait so long was that a lady who had surgery ahead of Rodger was found to have esophageal cancer, and her procedure took much longer than expected. The medical team had to open a separate operating room for Rodger and have it cleaned due to the length of the lady's surgery.

One by one, each person came into the Operating Room cubicle to ask Rodger all the routine questions about his name, his date of birth, and what type of surgery was being performed. I gave several license plates to a group of workers who were standing in the hallway, as I explained the same story about the 70-TIMES-7. They loved it and were excited. One girl came in and was seemingly quiet. I gave her the plate and told her the story, and she quietly said, "Thanks". Automatically, I began to feel a bit fearful that she was offended or did not like it, and I told her she could give it to someone else if she would like. God spoke softly to let me know it would be okay and that was just the right person. She left the room and returned about 30 minutes later. She said, "God always lets me know what I need to know, and I needed this today". Again, my heart was so humbled and blessed, and again, I heard, **"Just trust me, love God."** Rodger then kiddingly said, "If you will go ahead and give out all those plates, we can get surgery over with sooner." He knew in his heart as well as I knew, God would orchestrate who received them and when.

An anesthesiologist came in to introduce himself and let us know he would be with Rodger during surgery. After he asked the routine questions, I gave him a license plate and the story. He said, "Well, I just got engaged and might like to visit you two for pre-marriage counseling". We told him that would be great and gave him one of our ministry business cards. Even if he and his fiancé decide not to come, the forgiveness seed for marriage was planted. Forgiveness is always needed in marriage. We stayed back in the prep room so long that we saw two shifts of workers coming and going. To pass the time and stay strong, I began to quietly sing praise choruses to Rodger. Just as I began singing, "Way Maker, miracle worker, promise keeper," my phone dinged. Our youngest daughter sent us a photo of a beautiful rainbow. She said," I am outside and it's not raining, do you see the rainbow"?" We knew that was ordained by God at just that moment to give us hope, strength, and remind us of God's promises.

We met more Operating Room nurses and another anesthesiologist. We met one nurse who was so happy to receive the plate. She mentioned what a needed thing in our world today, and I reminded her that my dad had those made in 1993, and yes, perfect for today as well. Each one who was helping with Rodger's surgery, including the oncology surgeon and plastic surgeon, received a license plate and heard the story. There was one license plate left, and I was thinking of who would get it, as I figured we had met everyone there was to meet. Soon after, another lady come in who said she was taking the place of another worker who had gotten off work. I gave her the last license plate I had in my bag, told her the story, and thanked her for helping with Rodger's surgery. She was also excited to receive her gift. Within three to five minutes, Rodger was off to the Operating Room at approximately 6:30PM! Rodger looked at me and again, he kiddingly said, "I told you if you had given all those license plates away five hours ago, we would be home by now." He knew in his heart just as I knew that God had orchestrated the day just like He wanted things to be, and His timing is always perfect. Praise!

The waiting began and my heart was broken that Rodger had to go through this surgery, but the reality was that he needed the surgery, and God would be with both of us every step of the way! One of the nurses was leaving for the day and went by me carrying his bookbag and told me to look! There was the license plate showing through the mesh in his bag. He was proudly carrying it for everyone to see! God just kept blessing my heart through these people and their happiness about receiving the license plates.

One of the nurses was leaving the Operating Room for the day and came by the waiting room to thank me again for her license plate and wanted to let me know surgery had begun at 7:15 PM. I was relieved to know it was underway, but I felt a rush of emotions and tears. It is so hard to explain how you can be so comforted but the next minute be so unsettled and anxious. The enemy tried to keep me upset, but God calmed my heart again and gave me peace.

****

"Do not be anxious about anything, but in everything, by prayer and petition, with thanksgiving, present your requests to God. And the peace of God, which transcends all understanding, will guard your hearts and your minds in Christ Jesus." (Philippians 4:6-7).

****

I knew prayer warriors were praying for us because I felt the comfort from those time and time again as I waited. We cannot get that peaceful feeling under these conditions without the power of God in our lives and prayers. One by one, everyone had left the waiting room, and there I sat. At 8:00PM, a lady came by to tell me I would have to leave the waiting room by 9:00PM because the waiting room would be closed due to visiting hours being over at that time. I looked at her and said that I would just wait in the hallway or outside. She said "No, you will have to leave the hospital and go to a hotel or go home." I explained that my husband was having surgery and I did not want to leave him. She then said she would see what she could do. Meanwhile, at 8:15PM, the oncology surgeon came in to let me know his part of the surgery was over and things went as he expected. He removed one lymph node, as well as the wicked fast-growing melanoma. Those were his exact words. He said he did not really see anything with the naked eye that surprised him or looked strange, but we would have to wait for a week or so to receive the biopsy reports. He explained that he had to remove some cartilage from the ear which would require a skin graft and the plastic surgeon was completing his portion of the surgery as we spoke. Then he said the best words ever to my ears, "He can go home tonight." He did not have to stay overnight in the hospital! Those words were a huge answer to prayer, as I had asked several prayer warriors to pray for that specifically! I mentioned to the surgeon about having to leave the waiting room at 9:00PM, and that I did not want to leave Rodger. He told me to give him a few minutes. Within five minutes, a nurse came to get me and took me downstairs to the information area to obtain a special hospital pass with my photo identification that allowed me to be in the hospital until time to go home. What a praise! I had a chair in the hallway right outside the Operating Room to sit and be comfortable. God provided for even the smallest things even though staying until Rodger's surgery was over was a huge deal to me and not small and was a result of all the wonderful people praying.

Around 9:30PM, the plastic surgeon came out to let me know everything went as planned, and that he took skin from Rodger's collar bone area to graft to his ear and showed me a photo of the ear. Not that having a full ear left was the most important issue we were dealing with, but it felt awesome to see he had an entire ear left intact. Even though I could not totally see with the surgical dressings and medication on the ear, I trusted the surgeon who said he would see us in his office soon.

We left the hospital around 11:00PM, stopped at Walgreens to get his pain medication, and arrived home after midnight on Friday morning, August 28. It felt so good to be home. I had been awake for 21 hours and got about three hours of sleep that night, but God gave me so much energy that was unreal, and some said it was adrenaline. Either way, I had the strength and energy needed to take care of Rodger and then some. He was uncomfortable as he tried to find a position and place to rest. He initially resisted his pain medication, but I was eventually able to persuade him otherwise. He needed to stay ahead of the pain.

On Sunday, August 30, a special friend called to let me know she had placed something in our mailbox. It was a beautiful card and a CD. She remembered me telling her the story of the special number in our family 121 and this CD was by a contemporary artist with Psalm 121 as the main part of the title. I was so overwhelmed by her thoughtfulness I teared up and went upstairs where Rodger was resting to share with him. He teared up as well. Later in the day as I was listening to the CD, I felt impressed to call one of my cousins who I know is from a family of prayer warriors. As soon as she answered the telephone, she mentioned the pandemic and trying to stay well and then she mentioned Psalm 121! She told me her Bible was open to Psalm 121 all the time as it was precious scripture to her. I nearly fell out of my chair and could not believe my ears. I knew I was supposed to call her and ask her and her family to pray for Rodger and that was confirmation. God blessed me as we chatted, and I felt God moving as we shared with each other that day. "Look at God, honey," as our youngest daughter says. He just keeps giving me confirmation!

Rodger seemed to turn the corner of feeling better on Monday, August 31. He looked more himself and had no pain even though he had not rested well, so it was a time of praise to God! However, on Tuesday, we seemed to be back to not such a great day. He just could not get comfortable anywhere in the house to rest, and it made for a long day. Maybe he was feeling apprehension about the biopsy reports and just the uncertainty of his situation which is a very human reaction. Even though it was not the best of days, he rested five hours Tuesday night and that was such a huge praise!

On Wednesday morning, I awakened, anxious and apprehensive, and I got ready for Rodger's appointment with his plastic surgeon in Chapel Hill. I knew in my heart so many prayer warriors were praying over both of us, and I began praying. God is so faithful if we just trust in Him, and he gave me such peace and encouragement to my mind and soul.

****

"So do not fear, for I am with you; do not be dismayed, for I am your God. I will strengthen you and help you; I will uphold you with my righteous right hand." (Isaiah 41:10).

****

Using our common sense, we left early for our appointment and what a great idea. We encountered a 20-minute delay with a serious car crash about 30 minutes from Chapel Hill. I was the designated driver of the day and that rattled my nerves, but I stayed focused and arrived right on time with not a minute to spare. Rodger had the Glasscock, the white bowl, and the barrier that was sewn in place to protect the skin graft along with the gauze removed from his ear. Let me just pause here and say my husband is a serious trooper because he handled the pain well even though the medical team was wonderful, and they did what needed to be done. Just as we were told after surgery, we heard on this appointment day that his ear was completely intact minus some carti-lage, and the ear looked awesome! The plastic surgeon explained that this was serious surgery and a major deal, but the ear and the other two incision sites looked great. However, he said a lot of times he sees patients a week or two after this type surgery and the skin graft site will look healthy only to fall apart by the next office visit. Fall apart! That is about what I did when I heard that news. He told us to continue doing the same routine we had done the previous week since surgery and see him in a week.

****

"When I am afraid, I will trust in you." (Psalm 56:3).

****

Many times, over the last 20 years, we have made it a priority to daily put on the full armor of God to fight the attacks that come from the enemy. After our armor is on, we bind the enemy and loose blessings, not through our power but through the power of Jesus, through His blood, according to the Word of God, and by the Spirit of God. We have surely continued this routine most especially during these trying days.

****

"I will give you the keys of the king-dom of heaven; whatever you bind on earth will be bound in heaven, and whatever you loose on earth will be loosed in heaven." (Matthew 16:19).

****

On September 4, we hoped to receive the pa-thology results of the lymph node biopsy and the results of whether the melanoma margins were clear. Honest-ly, I felt so anxious and my patience level was waning.

Rodger noticed and mentioned our faith needed to stay strong. We continued to feel the prayers of all the faithful prayer warriors and knew God was in control, but this was hard. That morning, a popular song came on a Christian radio station that reminded me that nothing will shake me from his love because He is my high tower and deliverer. I sang the song to calm my anxiety. I prayed for God to give peace and help me not listen to negative thoughts the enemy whispered in my mind.

What a wonderful song to remind us that God is the same yesterday, today, and tomorrow, no matter what changes in our lives, and no matter if we are on the mountaintop or in the valley. We will trust in him, stand in faith, and not be shaken! The God on the mountain is still the God in the valley!

At 12:21, Rodger received a call from his surgeon as he was upstairs working in his office. I was downstairs staying busy cooking and doing other things to keep my mind busy. I was on a heightened sense of alert to whether he received a text or call with results. Every ding I heard on his telephone, I would go to the bottom of the stairs and ask, "Was that the oncology surgeon's office?" When I heard the telephone ring, I ran up the stairs hoping it was THE CALL. I heard Rodger say the words, "That's great news!" I immediately burst into tears of joy and praise to our Lord!! The surgeon told Rodger the pathology report was clear on the lymph node and clear margins from the melanoma that was removed during surgery. He said no treatments or scans were necessary. He confirmed we were scheduled to see him in his office on September 14. We were both filled with emotion as we both cried and loved each other. I ran outside to give a praise run on the street in front of our house in the cul-de-sac as I had told a few of the ladies in our neighborhood I would whenever we got the "praise" call! Now was the time to run and praise Jesus! It felt so awesome to hear this awesome news and to give God praise! Honestly, we both felt so overwhelmed by God's love, grace, mercy, and His peace that we were both sort of numb. I just sat and stared into space for a few minutes, and Rodger asked me if I was okay. I told him that I was just overtaken by emotions and so in awe of God.

****

"Consider it pure joy, my brothers, whenever you face trials of many kinds, because you know that the testing of your faith develops perseverance. Perseverance must finish its work so that you may be mature and complete, not lacking anything." (James 1:2-4).

****

God grew our faith through this journey, and we are forever grateful for the cross and for Him! As I type this, I have tears in my eyes and am so humbled. Thank you, Jesus!

Saturday morning was such a blessing and feelings of excitement for both of us because Rodger felt ready to take a short walk and it was 10 degrees cooler than it had been all summer. When the mandatory quarantine started in March 2020, we began working out at home as opposed to the gym since it was closed, and we walked each day about two miles in our neighborhood. We enjoyed that time together and had missed the walking since his surgery ten days prior. He was instructed to not lift anything over five pounds until told differently so working out would have to wait a bit longer.

As we waited to see how Rodger's ear skin graft was healing at his appointment with his plastic surgeon on September 9, we prayed so hard it would be good news. God has been so faithful, and we praise His Name! *Lord, we give you thanks, praise, and glory for your blessings and your love and mercy!*

****

"Whoever gives heed to instruction prospers, and blessed is he who trusts in the Lord." (Proverbs 16:20).

****

****

"We live by faith, not by sight." (2 Corinthians 5:7).

****

****

"The LORD is my strength and my shield; my heart trusts in him, and I am helped. My heart leaps for joy and I will give thanks to him in song." (Ps. 28:7).

****

Our hearts were overflowing with praise to Jesus as we left the plastic surgeon's office on September 9! He said the ear graft looked much better than he expected! However, he said there was one tiny place in the ear canal which was not directly connected to the skin graft and there was a breakdown in a small area of the tissue. We prayed diligently over this area, that it would show improvement by the next week when we would return for another checkup. There was one additional praise that the Glasscock was now gone, and he would no longer have to sleep elevated! Praise to Jesus and all prayer warriors who lifted Rodger to our Heavenly Father!

Over the summer of 2020 and into the fall, God blessed us with the opportunity to facilitate pre-marriage counseling couple counseling, single counseling, (all outside on our screened porch due to the Pandemic) and telephone counseling. We also received such sweet blessings from continuing to share many of the 70-TIMES-7 (forgiveness) license plates as a reminder of forgiveness as God randomly brought these people into our path. We know these license plates are connected to our lives not only through our marriage ministry and our desire to see people know about forgiveness, but also our day to day desire to tell everyone about His plan of salvation, mercy, and grace and faithfulness! God has been so faithful to us!

On September 14, we stood in faith and trusted as we headed to see Rodger's oncology surgeon for the first time since his surgery. I told Rodger as I look back over our valleys, worry never changed a single thing, but prayer has changed so many things in our lives. I did not rest well the night before, with so many things on my mind, and I was so tired and so concerned, (that is better than worry since I just told Rodger that worry had never changed anything), but I chose prayer and gratefulness for all the things God has done. The oncology surgeon thought his ear looked great and appeared to be healing well. It was his opinion that the tissue breakdown area looked okay, but we would confirm with the plastic surgeon on Wednesday. He said Rodger needs to be checked by his dermatologist every three months and he would see him every six months. The surgeon stated the melanoma was a stage 2 and could come back in the same or general area, so they want to stay on top of things as soon as possible. There is only a 25 – 30% percent chance of a recurrence. We praise the Lord for a good checkup and intend to follow all protocol for as long as necessary.

On September 16, we saw Rodger's plastic surgeon again, and he said Rodger had healed better than he had hoped, and his skin graft had healed better than most especially for his age! He said the tissue breakdown at the outside of the ear canal was almost healed and looked much better. There are a few places still healing as well! God is good and we give Him praise and glory! Rodger was told he can now return to his normal activities which, of course, includes workouts and golf. We were very teary and emotional thinking of all God has done for us both during this journey. We are also deeply appreciative of all the prayer warriors who have prayed for both of us! *Thank You Jesus!*

We returned to Chapel Hill to see the plastic surgeon on September 23, and he was amazed, yet again, to see how well the ear was healing. As of that day, the ear was approximately 95 percent healed, and the prognosis for complete healing was excellent! On October 7, we went back to the plastic surgeon for what we prayed would be our final visit. Praise the Lord, Rodger's ear was totally healed, and he was released!! We give all the praise and glory to our Lord Jesus Christ!!! **GOD IS SO GOOD!**

Study and Reflection

- Have you faced trying times over the course of life? Take a few moments to reflect and write them down.

- Can you recall how God sustained you and walked you through the events that took place? List some of ways that God was there for you, even in your trial.

- As we all know, not every sickness has a happy ending and grief is sad, hard, and can be emotionally heart-wrenching. Lazarus, who Jesus raised to life from the dead, eventually died again. Even in death, if that person had a personal relationship with Jesus, we rejoice that they are with the Lord. While there is a major sense of loss, if we have that same personal relationship with Jesus, we know that one day we will be reunited with our loved ones. It never takes away our grief for our loved one, but it gives us hope. God's Word tells us in Psalm 34:18 the Lord is close to the brokenhearted. He loves each of us and wants to comfort us in our times of grief.

- Have you accepted Jesus as your Lord and Savior? If not, invite him into your life and you will be forever changed. You can refer to the prayer of salvation we mentioned earlier in Chapter 2.

CHAPTER 7

More Unexpected

Just as we got in the car on September 9 after visiting the plastic surgeon and getting such a great report about Rodger's ear, I began sending out an update to all our prayer warriors to give praise to our Lord and Savior. About five minutes later, our oldest daughter, Heather, called to give us more unexpected! She had been having several health issues and scheduled an appointment to see her gynecologist. Heather was told there were several possibilities of which one could be cervical cancer! *What? God, our hearts are so heavy, and again, we cry out to you! Lord, please be with Andy and Heather and give them peace and comfort as they await testing and biopsies. Is this happening?* We both felt a rush of emotion and somewhat fear, but through it all, we had learned to trust in Jesus, and we would again. I could not hold back the tears. We were so grateful for Rodger's awesome news but so anxious to hear about Heather's questionable health. What a mix of emotions! We began praying fervently for her and her health situation.

I did not rest well that night as I tossed, turned, and prayed asking God to be with all of us as we would go through yet another period of waiting. The Holy Spirit spoke to my heart during the early morning hours as I was drifting in and out of rest saying, "You will go through the fire, but you will not get burned." I remembered the scripture in Isaiah 43:2-3 which states the same message. The next day, I gathered 15 of the crosses I had made for Rodger and took to share with Heather as I was scheduled to keep our grandsons that day. She placed them around their home just as we had done for Rodger in the areas which she would be in most each day. We told her to ask Jesus for healing over her health just as we would be doing for her.

****

"Do not let your hearts be troubled. Trust in God; trust also in me." (John 14:1).

****

****

"The LORD is my shepherd, I shall not be in want. He makes me lie down in green pastures, he leads me beside quiet waters, he restores my soul. He guides me in paths of righteousness for his name's sake." (Psalm 23:1-3).

****

That very same day, as I left Heather's house and began my journey home, our youngest daughter, Adrienne, called to let me know she had found another lump in her breast. I just stopped and asked God for His mercy, peace, and sustaining grace. *Lord, I love you, I praise you, I need you, I trust you, I do not know what to say, I need your love, I need your mercy, I need your peace. Jesus, Jesus, Jesus!* The enemy was trying to tear us all apart, but again we asked Jesus for His healing touch on both of our girls in Jesus's name! My emotions had overtaken me in my humanness. These were our girls, our sweet babies, and we love them dearly! *Dear Lord, please help us!* The tears flowed – again!

I previously stated "another lump" because approximately five years ago, Adrienne found a lump in a similar location and went to the doctor. They decided to watch to see if it grew. Sometime later, she found another one in the same area and went back to the doctor. They performed an ultrasound and could not tell exactly what they were dealing with, so they decided to do surgery. After both lumps were removed, the doctor stated there was no evidence of malignancy to the human eye, and the biopsies confirmed neither was cancerous. What a praise! However, they told her after surgery that these could grow back at any time. Maybe this was the same thing or not, but she scheduled a doctor's appointment for September 21 to have a mammogram and an ultrasound to confirm. I gathered several of the red crosses I had made and mailed them to her to place them in areas she would be close to each day and poured out our hearts to God over her health, just as we had done for Rodger, Heather, and now Adrienne!

****

"Peace I leave with you; my peace I give you. I do not give to you as the world gives. Do not let your hearts be troubled and do not be afraid." (John 14:27).

****

Tuesday, September 15, Heather, called to let us know she had completed her doctor's appointment. She confirmed she had never received any past abnormal test results which included the past year. Even so, her doctor decided to perform additional tests to see if there were any abnormal or cancerous cells present. The doctor also planned to complete an ultrasound within a month. Heather's bloodwork showed she was anemic, so she began taking some additional vitamins.

Adrienne called on the 21st to let us know she had completed her mammogram and ultrasound. With the radiologist right there in the room, they quickly confirmed there was no concerns of cancer, just two cysts!!

PRAISE THE LORD! Again, as Adrienne likes to say, "look at God, honey"! What a wonderful breath of air! We gave God praise and glory for His wonderful mercy and thanked Him that she is healthy!

****

"You are my God, and I will give you thanks; you are my God, and I will exalt you." (Psalm 118: 28).

****

We continued to anxiously await Heather's results and prayed for good news that all would be well. God, you are so good, and we love you and thank for your faithfulness. We praise your name! It is times in our lives like this that we need to know Jesus and lean on Him to comfort, give peace, and have faith to know we will be okay no matter what happens. The old Hymn came to mind, "Leaning on the Everlasting Arms," and that is exactly what we did! We leaned on His arms.

Friday, October 2, 2020, Heather called to let us know that her test was all clear as well as the biopsy; neither showed signs of cancer! PRAISE THE LORD! They planned to complete the ultrasound to confirm signs of cancer; however, we already believed all would be well. Wednesday, October 7 the ultrasound was completed, and they determined that there was what appeared to be a large cyst on the right ovary. Because of the cyst, there was concern it might be ovarian cancer; therefore, they completed a ROMA test. They stated the cyst must be removed regardless of the outcome of the test and scheduled a second ultrasound and recheck. Friday, October 9, Heather received a call that the ROMA test was negative, and no signs of cancer were found. Praise the Lord! Those were sweet words to our ears as we gave God praise and glory once again. As a compliment to traditional methods, Heather has been using natural foods, vitamins, and supplements in hopes of eliminating the need for any additional treatment or surgery. We continue praying that the cyst will be gone when she returns for her recheck. I immediately let Rodger know this awesome praise as we both had tears of gratefulness to our Lord for good health for both of our daughters!

As we close the sharing of our story, we understand that when your children are sick, you are challenged as parents to place your complete faith and trust in God and pray fervently for their healing. That is exactly what we did, and our hearts are so full of joy and thankfulness to God! There is no way to express in words the goodness of God.

Study and Reflection

-   Even if you know the Lord and have a personal relationship with Him, dealing with tough times can be challenging. He has given us many scriptures about praising Him always, in the good times but also the bad times, and that can be difficult. Can you think of a time when things did not happen as you wished, but you were still able to trust in Him and praise Him?

-   For those who do not know Jesus as their personal Savior, going through tough times must be truly unimaginable. Do you have a family member, friend, or coworker who is facing a difficult trial and they do not know Jesus? Will you pray for their salvation and their situation? Would you be willing to share the gospel with them? While their salvation may not change the outcome of their current trial here on earth, it will change the outcome of where they will spend eternity. List the names of those close to you who need Jesus as their Savior and pray for them each day.

CONCLUSION

Whether you are contemplating marriage, already married, or you plan to stay single, we pray you have been blessed in some way by the information presented in our book. Please keep in mind that our enemy, Satan, is roaming around seeking to steal, kill, and destroy. He wants to destroy you as an individual, your marriage, your family, and ultimately your church family. Be wise and on guard. Remember to always put on the full armor of God found in Ephesians 6:11 in order to take a stand against the enemy's schemes; the belt of truth, the breastplate of righteousness, the sandals of peace, shield of faith, helmet of salvation, the sword of the Spirit, the Word of God. God is for you!

****

"The thief comes only to steal and kill and destroy; I have come that they may have life and have it to the full." (John 10:10).

****

****

"What, then, shall we say in response to this? If God is for us, who can be against us?" (Romans 8:31).

****

If you are married, you cannot change your spouse; you can only change yourself. Focus on yourself, pray for your spouse, for your marriage, and for both of you to trust in God with all your heart. As we have already said, we are not perfect people, so we do not have perfect lives or perfect marriages. However, as Janet's dad use to say, we can strive for perfection knowing that we will only be perfected when we get to Heaven. Try to be the best self and best Christian you can be every day. Just trust in God to help you through the difficult days, the valleys, and continue trusting Him and thanking Him when you have the mountaintop experiences as well. God is faithful yesterday, today, and tomorrow! We feel that Andrae Crouch best expressed our thoughts and praise to our Lord Jesus Christ in his song that reminds us to trust Him through it all...the good, the bad, on the mountaintop, and in the valley. From it all, we learn to trust Him as we witness His grace to us.

Remember the title of this book in your daily walk with the Lord: Just Trust Me, Love God.

REFERENCES

Beckett, Jeff. Sermon, January 31, 1999, Salem Baptist Church, Apex, NC.

Frost, Brian. "Tick Tock Goes the Clock" Sermon, 9 August 2020, Providence Baptist Church, Raleigh, NC.

The Holy Bible, New International Version. Zondervan, 2018.

Suffield, Kittie. "Little Is Much When God Is in It." The Celebration Hymnal, 1997, p. 633.